*Some Account of the Design of the Trustees
for establishing Colonys in America*

hands, the Negroe Slaves being both dull &
careless & not capable of winding it with
that nicety which it requires. Wine also
has been tried by way of curiosity & succe
but the Indian Massacre & unhappy
division between the Proprietors & peop
occasiond that & all other improvements to
neglected. Vincent Page 15 to Pag. 19

Beyond South Edistow the Contin
is at present all desolate. There a Nati
of Indians called Yamasees formerly
dwelt amongst whom the English liv'd
dispersed in single Familys without so
much as fortifying their Houses, but in
the year 1715 the Indians destroyed al
the unfortified Settlements. The terror
which incursion has prevented the in
=tiling any of the Lands on the Contin
to the Southward of the Edistow not
standing the Yamasees & other India

Some Account
of the Design of the
Trustees
for establishing Colonys
in America

By James Edward Oglethorpe

Edited by Rodney M. Baine and Phinizy Spalding

THE UNIVERSITY OF GEORGIA PRESS

Athens and London

© 1990 by the University of Georgia Press
Athens, Georgia 30602
All rights reserved

Designed by Sandra Strother Hudson
Set in Janson with Shelley Allegro by
The Composing Room of Michigan, Inc.
Printed and bound by Thomson-Shore

The paper in this book meets the guidelines for permanence
and durability of the Committee on Production Guidelines for
Book Longevity of the Council on Library Resources.

Printed in the United States of America

94 93 92 91 90   5 4 3 2 1

Library of Congress Cataloging in Publication Data

Oglethorpe, James Edward, 1696-1785.
Some account of the design of the trustees for establishing
colonys in America / by James Edward Oglethorpe ; edited by
Rodney M. Baine and Phinizy Spalding.
p. cm.
ISBN 0-8203-1237-1
1. Georgia — History — Colonial period, ca. 1600-1775 —
Pamphlets.   2. Great Britain — Colonies — America —
History — 18th century.   I. Baine, Rodney M.
II. Spalding, Phinizy.   III. Title.
F289.O363 1990
975.8'02 — dc20   89-20639
                                                              CIP

British Library Cataloging in Publication Data available

IN MEMORY OF

James Augustus (Gus) Baine

February 10, 1873–May 19, 1932

Contents

Acknowledgments

FOR PERMISSION to publish Oglethorpe's *Some Account of the Design for establishing Colonys in America* we are indebted to the Tampa-Hillsborough County Public Library, of Tampa, Florida, and especially to Mr. Joseph Hipp, curator of Special Collections, who made numerous photocopies of the manuscript for us and helped, during our visit there, to make possible a close reading. We are also indebted to the English and history departments of the University of Georgia for providing travel funds and typing. For this last we owe thanks to De Ann Palmer, Connie Perry, Peggy Lewis, Renee Wilson, Tina Locke, Pat Johnson, and especially Sheila Trembley. In various ways we are indebted also to Mills B. Lane III, of Savannah; John Reps, of Cornell University; Louis De Vorsey, professor emeritus of geography at the University of Georgia; and to John Camp, curator of Special Collections at the University of South Florida. For permission to reproduce some of the material in "James Oglethorpe and the Early Promotional Literature for Georgia" we are grateful to *William and Mary Quarterly*.

Rodney M. Baine assumes primary responsibility for editing *Some Account* and for Section II of the introduction, regarding problems of authorship; Phinizy Spalding, for Section I, which suggests the significance of Oglethorpe's text and attempts to place it in historical context. From the inception of our edition, however, we have worked together throughout the whole.

Introduction

IN A LETTER written by Governor Robert Johnson of South Carolina to James Oglethorpe in September 1732, the American colonial leader offered his advice to the man who, more than any other, was responsible for the movement to establish a colony south of the Savannah River. Bring over, he counseled, "none but people used to Labour and of Sober Life and Conversation." A different sort, he continued, "will never be govern'd nor make good Settlers." One distress after another, Johnson said, would attend the first arrival of new colonists in America — distresses "which will not be born by people used to Idleness or Luxury, and so far from being thankfull for the bounty bestowed upon them, will be discontented and mutinous."[1] Although this message crossed the ocean from Charles Town to London in just over two months — a reasonable passage for those days — Oglethorpe was not at the Georgia Office when Johnson's words from the southern frontier were received. Roughly one month earlier, Oglethorpe and his first settlers had dropped down the Thames River and had sailed from Gravesend on the ship *Anne.*[2] For better or worse, for permanency or for transience, the Georgia experiment was under way.

Had Johnson been fully aware of the situation in England his doubts might have been allayed. The Georgia idea had not been implemented without a great deal of thought; Oglethorpe had sailed from England well informed of the theoretical problems of colonization. In fact, when the pamphlet that follows this introduction is examined carefully, it may occur to the reader that Oglethorpe knew perhaps too much; his theory may have been ahead of his practice or, as Robert Browning might have said, his reach. Where, it could be asked, is the happy medium in such a circumstance? In effect, how balance theory with experience? — a question many have tackled, but few have solved. Any satisfactory response to such a challenge must depend, as always, on the situation and on the leader involved. Much is known about Oglethorpe — at least the public figure — once he assumed responsibility in Georgia. And, thanks to recent research, a good deal more is being pieced together about Oglethorpe's interests before and after the Georgia phase of his long and distinguished career. His family, his early military exploits, his ability as a publicist, his final campaigns in Europe in the 1750s when he fought under a nom de guerre, his marriage, and his associations with the Johnson-Boswell circle are all subjects currently under scrutiny.[3] It is curious, though, that little new information has been discovered on the subject that touches Oglethorpe the author and colonial theorist. With the publication of this booklet and with the identification of Oglethorpe as the author of other imperial tracts and pamphlets as well, Georgia's leader takes an additional stature and begins to assume his proper place as an equal with even the most prominent of the seventeenth-century founders of American colonies.

On the basis of hard evidence presented in the second half of this introduction, it appears indisputable that Oglethorpe was the author of *Some Account of the Design of the Trustees.* Therefore, and in light of the information accumulating that shows Oglethorpe to have been even more active as a colonial publicist than most scholars and biographers have thought in the past, it seems pertinent and necessary to ask why *Some Account* is significant for a fuller understanding of the planting of Georgia. Additionally, it should be useful to probe into the ramifications of that particular event.

Some Account reflects a well-educated, well-read, sensitive mind. Classical references abound as does documentation of sources — something of a rarity for eighteenth-century writing on American topics. For a man who could dash off a Latin poem with aplomb and who, in later life, was to have the gall to debate politics and ideas with Samuel Johnson,[4] mere documentation was no special problem, particularly when evidence indicates that Oglethorpe held in his personal library most if not all of the books to which he made reference.[5] In fact, the lengthy quotations and at times unnecessary footnoting make several sections of the pamphlet a trifle turgid — rather like an anxious academic showing off for his senior colleagues. Although he had authored pamphlets before that aimed to shape public opinion, notably *The Sailor's Advocate* in 1728, *Some Account* was his first serious venture into the complex world of American colonial theory. He must have spent endless hours poring over key sections of his discourse, and, probably nervous about the work's reception at the hands of a critical public and his even more critical Georgia associates, he buttressed his points with learned citations to fend off the dubious and the doubting.

But it is not the segments dealing with Roman and Greek colonization that are the most important in this pamphlet. Oglethorpe shows in *Some Account* a sensitivity to the southern frontier that few, if any, contemporary writers could match. It is obvious that Oglethorpe knew John Barnwell's ideas concerning fortified outposts and settlements in the back areas, and that he was also conversant with Governor Johnson's township plan, which had been taken up before the Board of Trade in 1730. He obviously had read John Oldmixon, and he had absorbed Joshua Gee; he most certainly knew Sir Josiah Child and Charles Davenant's works. As for the distant past, the tract shows him to be an admirer of Greek and Roman colonization projects, particularly the latter. He applauded Rome's ability to hold its borders and appreciated fully the empire's incorporation of colonial peoples and their ideas into the Roman mainstream.

More important for Oglethorpe and for the settlement he was to lead, he shows a keen awareness of the problems Carolina had labored under for several decades; he was determined that Georgia would not suffer from these same difficulties. He was troubled by American land speculation, the rapid growth of the institution of slavery, and the luxury and vice which that institution bred. In this light trusteeship Georgia can be looked upon as a sort of reverse Carolina: the warning signals that brought the older province to its knees in the Yamasee War and thereafter are clearly noted in *Some Account*. Oglethorpe's and the Trustees' subsequent actions in expressing their unique and sturdy rules for Georgia appear a natural outgrowth of these concerns.

To mention only a few points. Oglethorpe maintains that relations with the Indians had — at least for Britain — been more than just satisfactory in Carolina's early years. But the "extortion and violence" of the traders ruined these relations and the upshot was the Yamasee War — a conflict that set Carolina's affairs, and hence England's, back substantially. The Yamasee War played havoc and "many negligent Planters perished." Although defeated, the Indian uprising had caused such "terror" in South Carolina that its borders were wide open to Spain and France.[6] Georgia's settlement, he writes, would keep South Carolina's black slaves "in awe," and would calm the trauma felt by the older colony, particularly when it trembled at the horrid prospect of a concerted Negro-Indian alliance.

By the time this pamphlet was written it must have seemed

evident to Oglethorpe that the problem with the natives went beyond the surface relations between them and the aggressive British traders on the frontier. At the core of the difficulty was a system in Carolina that not only condoned fraudulent and dishonest trading but also lavished enormous land grants upon a certain favored few in its midst. The pattern of large landholding that had developed by about 1715 resulted in vast stretches lying vacant and defenseless, all but asking for an invasion by Britain's enemies. Speculation was rife; merchants, planters, and Indian traders jockeyed for positions of preference, first with the all-but-moribund proprietors, and later with the first royal officials to be appointed for Carolina.[7]

In *Some Account*, Oglethorpe is clearing a colonial path that he hopes will lead his new colony in a direction quite different from that followed by South Carolina. He is projecting a land system as yet untried on the American scene; most of the guidelines that ultimately resulted in the exotic fifty-acre tail male grants can be found in this early tract. Oglethorpe had resolved that Georgia would not repeat the system found in Carolina or other southern continental provinces. The reader can almost hear the author's thought processes at work as he dictates the outlines of his thinking on the question of the disposition of land as well as on the articulation of a well-balanced Indian policy.

Oglethorpe is groping, in this tract, for a solution to the age-old problem of relations between the natives and the English, especially with regard to issues concerning trading goods and appropriate procedures to be followed in the backcountry. At this stage in his colonial experience it appears that he has no advanced notion of the sort of legislation — if, in fact, legislation was to prove the panacea — needed to keep both traders and natives in a peaceful relationship with one another, and with England. It is probably correct to say that Oglethorpe arrived in America without having evolved clear-cut concepts of Indian society. Dealing with the natives at firsthand made him realize that the gross abuses characteristic of the trade, as carried on by the Carolinians and the Virginians, had to be ended. Oglethorpe proved to be an adept diplomat, and the evidence that he and others have left behind indicates his admiration for the structure of Creek and Cherokee societies. He seemed, furthermore, once exposed to the natives, to enjoy their company.[8] He was fascinated by their stories, and their religion appealed to him. The word of Oglethorpe's simpatico spread throughout Indian country, and delegations from even the far-off Choctaws and Chickasaws came to meet him. It most certainly was during the period of his earliest colonial apprenticeship that Oglethorpe decided to protect these tribes in the backcountry, if such a thing were in his power. He saw such a step as being in England's best interest, of course, but he also admired these straightforward people as individuals. His return to England in 1734, accompanied by Tomochichi, mico of the Yamacraws, and the chief's queen and heir, sealed his respect. As the natives were impressing England with their mellifluous speeches and their quiet dignity, Oglethorpe and the Trustees were putting the finishing touches on the Indian Act of 1735, designed to put Georgia officials in decisive positions in the backcountry. Carolinians, Virginians, or any other colonial traders would have to secure licenses to trade with "Georgia" Indians from Oglethorpe himself or from men he handpicked for the job. As a general rule, such licenses had to be renewed each year in Savannah, bond had to be posted for good behavior and adherence to Georgia's regulations, and "that demon Rum" — the favored item in the old trade — was expressly forbidden in the backcountry.[9]

It seems apparent from a reading of the following piece that its author has some serious questions in his mind about black slavery. At the time of the writing of *Some Account*, Oglethorpe still had an official association with the Royal African Company, but the reader can perhaps sense a change of approach in the author's thinking. With his emphasis on the military posture the colony must take, with his insistence upon limited landholding with inheritance strings attached, and with his strong aversion to Carolina society, it would seem that the prohibition of slavery in Georgia was a logical, sensible step to insist upon. In his drive to make sure that Georgia would not be another Carolina he recognized the intimate relationship between large grants, land speculation, slavery, and staple crops. But similar to the situation with the Indians, it took an on-the-spot inspection of the realities of life in South Carolina to convince him what he must do. A trip to Charles Town and some of its outlying dependencies in the spring of 1733 showed him the actuality at firsthand,[10] and once back in England he and his allies pushed for and secured the passage of the Negro Act. Such legislation as this, and the Indian and Rum Acts as well, is presaged in the passages of *Some Account.* All ordinances and legislation ultimately expressed by the Georgia Trustees touching upon land distribution, rum, the Indian trade, and slavery stuck firmly in the Carolina craw and were destined to pit these colonies against each other as long as Oglethorpe and his restrictions held the field.[11]

Apparently *Some Account* also helped Oglethorpe decide on the kind of site he wanted for his colony. Although his mind was probably already made up as a result of his own reading, observation, and past military experience, this pamphlet finds Oglethorpe for the first time delineating precisely the sort of location to be chosen by the leader of the province of Georgia. The spot must be north-facing, have good air and drinking water, be defensible, be accessible to ready water transportation, and not be near the miasmic marshes. This is a perfect description of the Yamacraw Bluff site on the Savannah River, picked by Oglethorpe for Georgia's first settlement with the approval of the resident chief, Tomochichi. Unfortunately there are no solid hints in this booklet as to the origin of Oglethorpe's strikingly effective urban plan for Savannah. His admiration for the Romans and his penchant for the military life might indicate the genesis of the Savannah layout, but we lack final evidence to prove any of the hypotheses concerning the basis of his ideas.[12]

In this booklet the reader senses Oglethorpe wrestling with the questions of the relationship of the established church — and other Christian sects as well — to the individual settler. The adherents of the Church of England were to be more closely regulated than followers of other faiths, and the role of the founder — patriarchal in tone — was carefully laid out on board ship. Oglethorpe, however, does not really go beyond a sort of general religious oversight in this essay. His opinion in the pamphlet, just as in the reality to come, was that the secular concerns of Georgia were paramount should they ever conflict with the spiritual.[13]

In fact, the reader of *Some Account* can almost see the colony of Georgia take substantive shape before his eyes. Beneath the surface of the entire social theory that provides Georgia's foundation is what Betty Wood of Cambridge has called a sincere and dedicated "concern with white virtue, white manners, and white morals." Oglethorpe and the Trustees sensed "the possible nature of the relationship between chattel slavery and the manners and morals of white society."[14] In Oglethorpe's tract this relationship is spelled out — sometimes laboriously, sometimes lugubriously. Moral purpose and reform of white society in Georgia might ultimately be transported back to England and provide the impetus for the desired changes that Oglethorpe and many of his colleagues deemed necessary to cleanse the mother country's body politic. The Trustees, with Oglethorpe at their head, had begun evolving a kind of enlightened, primarily secular Zion in America that would perform a function far greater than even the most san-

guine founders of other American colonies — the Puritans excepted — had dreamed possible for their provincial experiments.[15]

Oglethorpe set his goals high. He outlines in *Some Account*
precisely what the leader of this new and exotic colony of Georgia
should do. Although there is room to think that Oglethorpe is
trying to box rival philanthropist Thomas Coram into a corner
should he offer to lead the first settlers to America, there is equal
reason to believe that Oglethorpe was outlining the role he himself secretly wished to play. In this light he might be seen as draft-
ing himself for the role of founding father. Oglethorpe was not
shy and never hid his light under a bushel. He most certainly felt
competent to lead such an expedition. And, indeed, why should
he not?

How carefully Oglethorpe planned can be seen in his ideas concerning how the first transport should be organized and led. In
line with suggestions in his tract, eight of the Trustees assembled
at Gravesend on November 16, 1732, to muster the colonists
aboard and send them on their travels. On the voyage itself, Oglethorpe followed the procedures that he had suggested in *Some
Account*, although he seems to have relented from implementing
prayers twice daily. At least Thomas Christie, whose journal is an
important source for the *Anne*'s crossing, mentions only weekly
prayers, along with Dr. Henry Herbert's sermons on Sundays and
special days. But as Oglethorpe had suggested in the tract, he saw
to it that vinegar was used to swab the living quarters, that bedding was brought up to be aired, that the colonists were given a
plentiful and varied diet, and that the men were frequently exercised with firelock and bayonet. He also established rigid discipline, implemented his proposed basic social and political division
of tythings, and to enforce his insistence upon paternal authority,
when Mrs. Anne Coles beat her husband, he resorted for punish-

ment to the folk custom of skimmington. Throughout the voyage Oglethorpe acted in the paternal fashion he had suggested in his tract, so that before the colonists reached America, he had been accepted as the father image he projected in *Some Account.* Had this piece been intended for the stage, at its premiere Oglethorpe would have been listed as author, stage director, producer, and principal player all in one.

Some Account provides a basis for Benjamin Martyn and other pamphleteers to draw from in their later prose sketches of the Georgia blueprint. And it also gives an inside view of the developing ideas of philanthropy and white virtue as they relate to this new colonial experiment. In addition, Oglethorpe's piece contemplates a new way for English society and American colonizers to view Indian affairs, the institution of slavery, and the discriminating use of land grants by the Trustees.

Probably most important of all, though, this wide-ranging scheme for colonization gives the reader a new picture of its author. From these pages James Oglethorpe emerges as one of the most original leaders in Britain's imperial history. The image of Oglethorpe taking substance in *Some Account* is that of one of the best-informed Englishmen of his time in the field of colonial affairs. His plan for Georgia, a mixture of hard thinking, scholarship, philanthropy, experience, imperial enterprise, and idealistic theory, underscores this claim. *Some Account* will add to James Oglethorpe's already-established reputation as one of the most thoughtful philosophers of the first British empire.

II

Some Account of the Design of the Trustees for establishing Colonys in America has for many decades lain, almost unnoticed, in the Tampa-Hillsborough Library, in Tampa, Florida, incorrectly ascribed to Benjamin Martyn, the first secretary to the Georgia

Trustees.[16] However, as an examination of the manuscript and other contemporary documents shows, James Oglethorpe wrote the original draft probably during late 1730 and early 1731. He read the Tampa manuscript to the Bray Associates in early 1732, when it was somewhat revised. For various reasons it was never published.

The manuscript is a quarto of 110 pages, written on laid paper made in the Netherlands around 1732.[17] The leaves, which appear to be untrimmed, measure about 8 by 6¼ inches. Inside the cover is the purple bookplate of the Cholmondeley Library, but the coat of arms displayed there differs slightly from that of the marquesses of Cholmondeley or of the barons Delamere of Vale Royal.[18] There are no other marks to indicate previous or subsequent ownership.

Although the Preface, of nineteen manuscript pages, has been left virtually untouched, the text, of ninety-one manuscript pages, has been considerably revised, mostly in penciled interlineations and marginalia; several passages have been scored out; and extensive rearrangements have been indicated. The manuscript was apparently intended for publication but was incompletely revised — only the text through page 36. There is a formal title page, its verso blank. The Preface ends with a blank page. The text begins with a head title and ends with a "Finis." Topic headings like those which Oglethorpe had already used in his *Sailor's Advocate* (1728) have been penciled in the margins of pages 1–8, 22–29, and 33–35 of the text, but not beyond this point. There are lacunae left for the insertion of specific data and for two long quotations.[19]

Two hands appear in the manuscript: the original, in ink, is a careful Spencerian script; most of the revisions, in pencil, are in a different hand, sometimes scrawled; and in two passages, one or two words are almost illegible. Although time has done little to dim the ink, it has sometimes partly effaced the graphite. The Spencerian hand is that of neither Oglethorpe nor Martyn, though we would expect to see the latter's hand here if he were the author. During this period Oglethorpe was comparatively affluent and certainly quite busy, so we would not expect the fair copy to be his. He seems to have employed an amanuensis whenever he could, such as Luke Kenn in the prison investigations and the Wesleys and Francis Moore in Georgia. That the Spencerian hand is not that of the author is made clear from the copyist's query — "?where" — inked in the margin opposite the promise that how "the weaker and more helpless poor . . . may be made capable of subsisting themselves and be beneficial to the publick will be shown hereafter." He obviously expected to find the promise fulfilled further along in the pamphlet. The author was actually referring to the ease and simplicity of sericulture as delineated in Thomas Boreman's then unpublished *Compendious Account of the Silk-Worm*, which appeared in December of 1732, dedicated to Percival and the Georgia Trustees. The penciled script seems to be in the hand of Oglethorpe, but his habit of using a scribe whenever he could has left us few samples of his contemporary script with which to make comparisons.

It appears highly unlikely that Benjamin Martyn could have had anything to do with the writing or the revising of the manuscript. It nowhere shows his distinctive hand or his conventional pluralizing of nouns ending in *y*. Moreover the manuscript was completed and revised several months before Martyn arrived upon London's Georgia scene. The first reference to him as a prospect for the Georgia Trustees comes in their informal agreement on July 20, 1732, that he "would be a proper man" to act as their secretary.[20]

On the other hand, the evidence for Oglethorpe's authorship seems conclusive. On November 12, 1730, in Oglethorpe's absence, the Associates for D'Allone's Charity, who in May of 1731 became simply the Bray Associates, resolved "that a Treatise be drawn up in Order to be printed, to encourage all charitable Persons to contribute towards the charitable Colony intended to be fixed in some one of the American Plantations belonging to the King of Great Britain, and that Mr. Oglethorpe do prepare the same."[21] At the same meeting they adopted a policy for revision, "a standing Rule, that any Book drawn up by Order of these Associates to be printed be first perused by four Members successively, to be nominated by them at four Meetings, who are to make their Report of the same, and such Amendments as they shall think proper, and that afterwards the Book and Amendments be approved of or rejected by balloting."[22] In actual practice the rule was sometimes modified. On January 14, 1731, for example, a document was "perused at the same time by four several Members"—as the author read it aloud.[23] This was apparently the procedure followed in the revision of Oglethorpe's manuscript. On February 4, 1732, a few days after King George II gave his approval to a draft of the Georgia Charter, Sir John Percival recorded in his diary, "Met our Carolina gentlemen, and prepared a draft of an account of our design in order to be printed."[24] Percival was evidently not present during the entire revisal; perhaps he had already read the manuscript and felt that his presence would not be needed. The minutes of the secretary, the Reverend Mr. Samuel Smith, record the attendance of only Oglethorpe, in the chair, and the requisite four amenders: Stephen Hales, Adam Anderson, William Belitha, and Captain Thomas Coram.[25]

There also exists considerable internal evidence for Oglethorpe's authorship. Several quotations in the manuscript reappear in his *Select Tracts* (1732) and in his *New and Accurate Account of the Provinces of South-Carolina and Georgia* (1732) and seem to have been taken from books in his library. The extensive borrowings from Vitruvius are probably drawn from the unpublished translation of his friend Robert Castell. Moreover there are close parallels between *Some Account* and a letter that Oglethorpe wrote to Bishop George Berkeley in May of 1731. Three times in *Some Account* Oglethorpe quotes from Sir Walter Raleigh, whom he praised in *Select Tracts*, whose "journal" — *Discoverie of the . . . Empyre of Guiana* — he reportedly took with him on his first voyage to Georgia, and of whose *History of the World* he may have owned as many as five editions.[26] In *Some Account* almost two pages are reserved for a quotation from Machiavelli, several selections from whose writings appear in the *Select Tracts*, printed probably from Oglethorpe's copy of the *Works* of 1680.[27] Oglethorpe also quoted from Sir Josiah Child's "Discourse concerning Plantations," about half of which he reprinted in his *Select Tracts*, evidently from a copy of Child's *New Discourses of Trade* that he had in his library.[28]

Perhaps even more conclusive is the section of eight pages quoted from the Roman architect Vitruvius, whose *De Architectura* had just been translated by Castell. His manuscript translation was doubtless given or loaned to Oglethorpe by Castell's widow after the author died in prison on December 12, 1728. (It was Castell's death that soon led to Oglethorpe's drive for prison reform and to his colonization of Georgia.) Finally, the similarities between *Some Account* and the letter to Berkeley seem to confirm Oglethorpe's authorship. They are close, and details of the plan are listed in basically the same order. Some of the specifics are mentioned in our notes.

These parallels also suggest that Oglethorpe wrote much of his tract by May of 1731. A date before April 11, 1730, is suggested by a reference to the Peace of Utrecht in 1713: "Praise be to Heaven that there have been 16 [years] without any foreign War that could deserve the name." An early date is suggested also by

the concept of work rent expounded in *Some Account* and in the
letter to Berkeley, and by some of the terminology of the tract.
Oglethorpe several times refers to the petitioners as "the Charity," that is, the Associates for D'Allone's Charity. This style of
reference for the parent group became obsolete after May 1731,
when the charity group became simply "the [Bray] Associates." In
the revised part of the manuscript "the Charity" was invariably
penciled out and replaced by "the Trust" — the Georgia Trust.
Moreover, the scribe usually designated the new colony as part of
Carolina or South Carolina, as did the petitions from the Associates for D'Allone's Charity and the Bray Associates to the Board
of Trade during 1730 and 1731. Since only on January 27, 1732,
did King George II finally approve a draft of the Charter "for
Colony of Georgia,"[29] Oglethorpe may have been uncertain
about the fate and name of the new colony until a few days before
he handed the final draft to his amanuensis, so that he would have
a fair copy — the present manuscript — to present to the Bray Associates at their meeting scheduled for February 4. Nowhere, by
the way, did he or his revisers alter "Carolina" to "Georgia,"
although after one reference to the proposed location in "Carolina," Oglethorpe penciled "part of which his Majesty has Erected into a new Province by the name of Georgia." By February 5,
1732, the London papers were already using the name Georgia
for the new colony.[30]

But because of the three inked references to "Georgia" in the
latter part of the manuscript, the final draft must be dated after
April 11, 1731, probably after October 9, 1731, and possibly even
as late as January 27, 1732, or a few days thereafter. On the first of
these dates Captain Coram's long-cherished dream of a colony of
Georgia in what is now the state of Maine came to an end with the
ruling of the attorney general and solicitor general that the region
belonged to the colony of Massachusetts Bay.[31] Since Captain

Coram did not contest the decision, the name now became available for the southern colony.[32] However Captain Coram himself probably did not use the name for the new colony until after October 9, 1731, for in his letter of that date to Governor Jonathan Belcher of Massachusetts he was apparently still calling the region Carolina or South Carolina.[33] Of course the three references to Georgia in the manuscript may be last-minute insertions. Perhaps when he learned in late January that King George had at last approved a charter for the province under the name of Georgia, Oglethorpe dusted off his last draft, made a few changes, and handed it to his copyist.

From the fact that the revision of the manuscript is incomplete and that the minutes of neither the Bray Associates nor the Georgia Trustees mentions it, we can infer that the process of revision ended inconclusively. Apparently the revisers reached a point where they were unable or unwilling to proceed. Although the causes of this impasse are not entirely clear, the difficulties that caused a permanent halt in the revision probably lay in the manuscript and in a rift between some of the revisers. The manuscript was too long for inexpensive distribution, and on many points it was unnecessarily controversial. Many of its detailed suggestions seem to have been directed not to potential settlers or benefactors, as the associates wished, but to the "overseer" of the new colony. It may have been Captain Coram who objected to some of the suggestions vigorously enough to stop proceedings, for on June 8, 1732, before the Bray Associates, who petitioned for the Georgia Charter, had officially become the Georgia Trustees, Coram presented to them "a Paper containing a Draft of the Designs of the Trustees," which probably replaced with proposals of his own the principle of tail male and some of the Roman and medieval characteristics of Oglethorpe's plan. With Oglethorpe in the chair, the associates politely but evasively agreed that Captain Coram's draft "be taken into further consideration."[34]

When Oglethorpe wrote his tract he probably did not expect to accompany the first Georgia settlers, the first "colony,"[35] and he may have feared that Coram, or perhaps some South Carolinian, might be their leader. Hence the specific nature of his directions. When he wrote to the Board of Trade and Plantations on December 7, 1730, concerning the proposed Georgia Charter and militia, he urged "that the Governour of South Carolina shall command the said Militia."[36] Although he later protested vigorously against the king's decision that "the governour also should nominate the inferior officers," he did not, even as late as February 25, 1732, object to the governor's command of the Georgia militia.[37] Moreover when he wrote to George Berkeley, in May of 1731, he apparently did not expect to go to Georgia. The Trustees, he wrote, "intend to send no governour to prevent the pride that the name might instill. The power of government they intend to invest in an overseer and council of honest and discreet men."[38] Meanwhile the Georgia Trustees were searching for a reliable "agent," presumably to be placed in charge of the first settlers. When on May 2, 1732, an English merchant applied to Percival for this position, Percival responded that "they knew a gentleman of that Colony [South Carolina] who was a proper man for to be our agent, and I thought a person settled there of long time was properer than a stranger to that country."[39] Perhaps Percival had in mind James de St. Julien, the South Carolina surveyor and planter whom Governor Johnson had apparently recommended to Oglethorpe. On September 28, 1732, Johnson wrote: "I do believe it would have been of great Service to the Design if such a Person as Mr St. Julian could have been prevailed upon to have taken the Direction of the first Transport, one who knows the Country and the manner of new Settling. . . . Undertakings of this nature require the Management here of those who know the Climate and manner of settling. . . . I hope the first Transport won't be given to the Management of a Stranger to

xxvii

Introduction

these parts and Settlements."[40] (Before Oglethorpe left Georgia for England in 1734, the Trustees placed temporarily in the hands of James de St. Julien and Francis Scott the very same executive powers which they had granted Oglethorpe.)[41] If Oglethorpe had indicated to Johnson that he expected to accompany the first colonists, the governor's advice would surely have been more tactfully phrased. When Oglethorpe finally announced to the Trustees that he was available, in October of 1732, Percival's reaction suggests that the news was unexpected: "it rejoiced me that Mr. Oglethorpe would go, for my great pain was that although we were ever so well prepared, it would be difficult to find a proper Governor, which post he has accepted of."[42]

On the other hand, Captain Coram had apparently let it be known abroad that he was available to lead the first group of settlers. In response to his letter of February 25, 1732, Governor Jonathan Belcher of Massachusetts replied, on April 24: "I observe you have some thoughts of going over with the settlers design'd for the new colony of Georgia in S° Carolina." Months earlier, on October 9, 1731, Coram must have made the same suggestion, perhaps adding that his wife, a former Bostonian, might accompany him; for in his response, the concerned Belcher warned, "I hope for your own & Mrs Coram's sake you'll think no more of that Carolina enterprize."[43] When Oglethorpe finally decided to go, he saw to it that Coram was informed among the first: it was the captain who informed Percival, then at Bath.

However, since Coram had apparently prevented the approval and publication of Oglethorpe's *Some Account*, the Trustees took the wise and politic course. Someone, probably one of Martyn's sponsors, either Robert Hucks or George Heathcote, evidently suggested to Martyn that he prepare a brief and uncontroversial abridgment of Oglethorpe's manuscript. Martyn obliged by writing a four-page appeal for contributions, a diplomatic pastiche of quotation and paraphrase from the charter and the manuscript,

completely avoiding such controversial issues as tail male. Then at
their meeting of August 3, 1732, the Trustees "directed that Martin's *short* account of the design of the Georgia Colony and the
advantages accruing from it to England should be printed" (our
emphasis).[44] In the Common Council, however, into which
Coram was never elected, the members expressed their confidence in Oglethorpe by continuing him as the director of the
promotional campaign for the new colony.[45]

Although Oglethorpe and the Georgia Trustees never published *Some Account*, its usefulness was not restricted to the quotations and paraphrases that appeared in Martyn's *Some Account of
the Designs of the Trustees for establishing the Colony of Georgia in
America* (1732) and *Reasons for Establishing the Colony of Georgia*
(1733). The function of its preface was even better served by
Oglethorpe's *Select Tracts;* and its text served as a quarry for his
*New and Accurate Account of the Provinces of South-Carolina and
Georgia.* Moreover, the material directed to the overseer never
needed publication because as the leader of the colony Oglethorpe put into practice the plan that he had embodied in his
manuscript. Some of the controversial suggestions were never implemented. The suggestion of one day's work each week as a substitute for rent, for example, had been a nugatory dream for more
than a year before the manuscript was finally revised by the Bray
Associates. Had they, in their revisal of the manuscript, reached
the discussion of work rent in lieu of quit rent, they would have
felt impelled to alter it, for they were in no position to make such
a commitment. But otherwise *A Short Account* served as a virtual
blueprint of the Georgia genesis. Its publication should help to
clarify the origins of the colony.

Throughout our edition we have omitted the catchwords at the
foot of each page of the manuscript and have modernized the use
of quotation marks, which in the manuscript usually begin each

tion*
tion

quoted line. Within the quoted material we have tried to reproduce the original, taking the liberty only of supplying a necessary period and expanding contractions indicated in the original by a stroke over an *m*. Elsewhere we have taken as our model Julian Boyd's edition of *The Papers of Thomas Jefferson* (Princeton, 1950–). We have spelled out the uncommon contractions and have normalized the common ones. We have retained the spelling, capitalization, and italicization. We have supplied periods inadvertently omitted, most of them at the end of a paragraph or a line; and we have added a few commas and semicolons, these only to prevent misreading. A long dash reproduces the line that Oglethorpe's scribe used in the quotations to indicate an omission, sometimes a considerable one. Spaced periods represent blank spaces left by the copyist for the insertion of specific data, or in one case for a long quotation. Brackets enclose letters or words, in roman, supplied by us. Where penciled revisions in the manuscript replace or expand canceled ink originals, we reproduce both versions, first the original, italicized and bracketed. (Neither spaced periods nor brackets appear in the manuscript.) Since in the infrequent inked revisions the scribe seems usually to have corrected his own mistakes, here we do not reproduce his canceled original version. We have not followed Oglethorpe's original order but reproduce the tract as it was revised for publication by him and his amenders, indicating these changes in our notes.

*Some Account of the Design of the Trustees
for establishing Colonys in America*

Preface

THE FIRST HONOURS of the ancient World were paid to the
Founders of Citys; they were esteemed as the Parents from whose
Wisdom whole Nations had their being and were preserved. The
people carried their Gratitude to excess, and for such actions
Romulus and Theseus were placed amongst the Gods. By such
great Spirits such Benefactors of Mankind the whole World was
filled with Inhabitants. All Countrys were first peopled either By
Migrations or Colonys. Of the former the people of Israel was the
most wonderfull example in History, Moses led a mighty Nation
out of misery and bondage, marched them for 40 Years through
Desarts and gave them Laws by which they were established in a
fertile Land. The People of Phocea, a Grecian City in Asia powerful at Sea, rather than submit to the Persian Yoke abandoned
their native City and trusting to the mercy of the Waves em-
barked with their Wives and Familys and after a Navigation of
. . . Leagues established themselves in Gaul where they founded
the City of Marsceilles, which soon grew more potent than that
which they had abandoned.[1]

The way of peopling by Colonys was very ancient and the great
City of Carthage it self was a Colony of the Phenicians. Many
were planted by the Egyptian Hercules of which time hath effaced
the very names.

The Grecians established Colonys very early and by it extended
their Fame and Language. Homer mentions that before the Tro-

jan War, the City of Pheacia was founded by a Colony of the Hyperians.

> Then great Nausithous from Hyperia far
> Thro' Seas retreating from the sound of War,
> The recreant Nation to fair Scheria led,
> Where never Science rear'd her laureld head:
> There round his Tribes a strength of Wall he raisd,
> To Heav'n the glittering Domes & Temples blaz'd
> Just to his Realms he parted Grounds from Grounds
> He shar'd the Lands & gave the Lands their bounds.[2]

From the single City of Athens were 12 Colonys planted in Asia most of which became equal to their Mother City in greatness and Athens at the same time increased in Power, Fame and number of Inhabitants.

After the Destruction of Troy the Grecians sent so many Colonys to Italy that the whole Eastern Coast of that Region was called Graecia Magna.

Theocles first discovered Sicily to the Greeks and leading thither a Colony of the C[h]alcidians built the City of Naxus.[3]

Syracuse was a Colony of the Corinthians led by Archias.

The Grecians sent forth Colonys as the Bees do Swarms and never thereby weaken the Hive: for the vacancys made by those who went off gave room for others to marry and beget Children. The people all married young, being secure of providing for their Children. Since if their own Countreys refused them sustenance there were new Colonys ready and those taking off Goods made by their native Citys, by increasing the demand of Manufactures increased the number of hands employed in them. This occasioned the Grecians to be exceeding populous *so long as they continued sending out of Colonys and after the Romans became powerful, and prevented them from* it, they were by degrees so depopulated that when Plutarch writ, all Greece could not furnish 2,500 free Men fit to bear Arms, though in their earlier times Athens only upon the Sicilian expedition put to Sea a Fleet of 130 Galleys 30 Transports, on board which were 5,000 *heavy* Armed and 6,000 *light* armed Citizens.

The Grecians when they sent forth Colonys established them free Citys under the same form of Government as their own and reserved no Dominion over them, being contented with providing for their poor, extending their Fame, Language and Commerce by the increase of consumption made by so many Persons enabled to live well and comfortably. Yet did some benefits arise from the Gratitude of their Colonys: The Syracusians when Xerxes with his huge Armys passed the Hellespont, for the relief of Greece armed 30,000 Soldiers and 200 Ships.[4] There was a perpetual intercourse of friendly Offices between the Colonys and the Mother Citys till both together sunk under the overbearing Arms of Rome.

The Romans reduced the establishing of Colonys into an Art and made that the basis of Universal Empire. This was their great Elixir and cure of all Political evils. If the oppression of Usurers and misery of the Debtor allarmed the City with Seditions, a sending forth of Colonys thined the multitude, relieved the necessitous and cured the discontents. If a hot aspiring Genius arose, the employing it in deducing a Colony, made that fire which might have destroyed serviceable to his Countrey.[5]

Their Conquests in Italy were maintained by Colonys and thereby they spared the expence and Danger of mercinary standing Armys. When the great Scipio was called out of Spain to invade Africa, not daring in those extreams to weaken his Army by leaving any strong Garrisons in Spain he formed Colonys of his Invalid Soldiers and incorporating them, founded Citys one of whom from Italy he called the Italian which many years after was famous for the birth of the Emperors Trajan and Adrian.[6]

These Colonys maintained Spain in Peace and in quiet submission to the Romans without the expence of an Army which the City could then ill spare and by this they avoided the misfortune that Hannibal fell into, who by leaving his Brother with choice Troops for the defence of Spain lost that force which if he had had in Italy, Rome it self must have sunk under the weight of his Arms.

Had the superfluous expences bestowed by Lewis the 14th on building the magnificent Hospital of Invalids been employed in establishing Colonys of his old Soldiers and had he given them leave to marry and Land to support their Familys in his new Conquests; he would not in his latter times have been reduced to those terrible extremitys for want of hands to till the Ground and carry on the War: for by Arithmetical Progression it is demonstrable that from the many thousand Invalids who by a forced celibacy died Childless in the begining of his Reign might have proceeded Children sufficient to have formed mighty Armys in the latter end of it. Had they had Lands they would have married and the Children born in Wedlock would have been reared and not exposed or destroyed as the fruits of a Criminal Conversation generally are.

The larger and more extended the Conquest is, the more the Conqueror is weakened by success and frequent Victorys must render him. To prove this, suppose a State Sovereign of a Country able to keep a hundred thousand Men in pay and to furnish 5,000 for their yearly recruits which may in times of Peace be sufficient. If this State should employ that hundred thousand Men in a victorious War they will be weakened by the Conquest, for that hundred thousand Men employed in War will require at least 30,000 yearly recruits to make up the ravage which the Enemy, Sickness and Fatigue have made, and those 30,000 Men must be taken from useful Employments at home. The publick Revenue will be lessened as much as is gained out of the labour of those Men, for the Taxes which support Government arise from the labour of the Subjects. As for the conquered Countrey, that being ravaged and laid desolate by War, will be very little able to add any thing to the wealth of the Conquerors. Besides if one hundred thousand Men were before necessary and that they have conquered a Countrey in extent and strength equal to their own, they must at least keep two hundred thousand in Arms and by that means lose the labour of one hundred thousand more Subjects to defend and keep in awe the newly subjected people who will naturally be averse to their Government. If according to the modern way the Soldier is unmarried and the rule holds that Males and Females are born in equal numbers, there will be near two hundred thousand Women without Husbands, and the State will lose the Children which would have been produced by so many Marriages.[7]

It has been proved by thousands of Examples, that Kingdoms are the weaker by Conquests and that the larger the conquered Countrys are, the more it weakens the conquering Nations. It has always this effect, sometimes it is felt immediately as the late King of Sweden experienced who conquered so fast that his Countrey unable to furnish him, he was forced to recruit from the conquered, and he at the Battle of Poultnay [Poltava] found too late that his Army no longer consisted of the brave Sweedish Nations. Sometimes the Wound rankles longer before it breaks out as in the case of Lewis the 14th who felt not so soon the weakness which the extending his Dominions occasioned. But after the Conquests of the Franche Compte, Alsace and Flanders recruits became every year more difficult, the Taxes every year more deficient and the Discipline of the Troops for want of pay and recruits every year relaxed. For a while the decay was patched up by the great Genius's of Louis Vauban and Luxemburgh, but when the War after the Peace of Reswick was renewed, the ulcerated Wound broke out, even the most populous Kingdom of France not being able to furnish Men for the numerous Garrisons and Armys which those extended Conquests required. His Troops through scarceness of recruits were strong upon Paper, weak in the Field; Battle upon Battle, Town after Town were lost, the more Men he drew from the Plow the more his Revenue decreased, and the Fields for want of hands being left untilled occasioned the Famine in the year 1710.

The Romans knew well how narrow the foundation of one City was to build a mighty Empire upon, they knew well if they went the common way to work that large Conquests would require large Armys and those Armys more recruits and Taxes so that in the end they must sink under the weight of their Victorys. They therefore established Colonys as Brutus says in his Oration to the People after the death of Caesar.

"When they had overcome their Enemys they confiscated not their whole Countrey but contented themselves with taking a part of their Lands which they divided amongst their own Invalids & on them built Citys for them to inhabit & keep the newly subdued People in subjection, but if the conquered Countreys were not sufficient to give a comfortable subsistance to the Colony they added either some of the publick Lands or Lands bought with the publick Money. They also out of the conquered Countrys set aside Rents for the publick Treasury." And Appian in another place says "The Romans when they conquered any People of Italy confiscated such part of their Lands as they thought convenient & to those they sent Colonys. Sometimes they gave the Citys they had taken ready-built to be inhabited by their own Nation: with these Colonys they Garrisoned the conquer'd Countrys & either set out in equal Shares to those new Inhabitants such Lands as were fit for tillage or else sold or let them to farm in equal divisions. Such Land as was laid waste by War or was uncultivated & therefore not proper to bear a part in the dividend, they proclaimed & gave to such as would improve it, on Condition to pay as an anual Tribute the 5th part of the increase of Trees & the 10th of Corn & a Duty upon all sorts of Cattle as well Flocks as Herds. By the establishing of these Colonys they strove to preserve the Roman & Italian Nations, a laborious race, that they might always have of their own People Soldiers to serve them in extremity."[8]

By the means of their Colonys they Garrisond their Conquests and increased their Revenue, so that no sooner was one War ended but they were fresh and vigourous for another. Nor was this the only advantage since hereby they increased the people, for the more employment there is for Men, the more Children will be begotten and the more Men they will be.

Very few but those who are exceedingly debauched would abstain from Marriage if they could be sure of subsistance for themselves and familys equal to their Estate. To encourage the desire of nature the Senate gave power to the Father over his Children till their Marriage and exemption from all services to the Parents of 3 Children, besides which they were sure that if their Children should be too numerous to earn their Bread at home, there would be a comfortable subsistance for them in the Colonys. These encouragements made the Men eager for Marriage and they solicited the Roman Virgins in so effectual a manner that it is remarked in the better ages of the Republick, that no Woman who was not deformed (the Vestal Virgins only excepted) ever lived to the age of 25 Years unmarried. The effects of the Colonys was such that the Roman people increased so wonderfully under all their Wars that when they were numbered in the 210th year from the building of the City they amounted only to 80,000 Citizens and being numbered about the 500th year they amounted to

297797. So that in the space of 290 Years the Citizens of Rome increased 217797 notwithstanding they were frequently afflicted with Plagues and Famine and were the whole time engaged in continual Wars with the Gauls, with Pyrrhus King of Epirus and with the Italian States all whom they in that Space *subdued*, and in those 290 Years they established above 18 Colonys who generally consisted of upwards of 6000 Familys each. I cannot omit this remark that the Roman method of establishing Colonys answered the end so well, that no one Colony ever rebelled, nor no one Province once conquered by Rome was ever seperated from it till the final division of the Empire.

Some Account of the Design of the Trustees for establishing Colonys in America

MANY POOR FAMILYS are reduced to the utmost necessity by inevitable misfortunes. As Tradesmen who have suffered losses, Artificers and Manufacturers of such branches of Trade as are decayed or overstocked, Fathers of numerous Familys by Sickness thrown behind hand so as they cannot retrieve it, Labouring men who having served in the Army or in private Familys when discharged are rendered by disuse incapable of returning to their former Occupations. Many by too much good nature to rescue others have undone themselves. The Prisons were full of these who were bound for others or ingaged in Law Suits. It is true that great numbers [*are*] have been and are Daly relieved by Parliamentary Compassion, a noble Charity but not intirely compleated, for those only who have friends to assist them can become beneficial to the publick whilst the Insolvent who is turned naked out of a Prison and has not a Friend to trust him with work reaps but the priviledge of starving at large.[9] The want of Friends, want of Credit or a false shame of working in a lower degree prevents several honest Men from being useful in England and makes them either perish for want, fly their Countrey or seek for

Poor Hoped People who can not gain a Subsistance in England

Bread by unlawful means. Want first reduces them to Sickness or to Prison, and when the Mans industry is useless the Wife and wretched Children must either perish or ask relief of their Parish which perhaps disowns them perhaps allows them enough to prevent their being famished to Death but not enough to prevent Sickness the constant Companion of Famine. The gay and rich part of Mankind were wholly unacquainted with the numbers of their fellow Creatures who languished and dyed through meer want till the late Committee of Inquiry when it appeared by the lowest Account that 300 Persons per Annum had at a medium for several years past perished in one Prison only.[10]

As there are some in England whom misfortunes may force abroad there are infinite numbers in other parts of Europe to whom Tyranny and Persecution have made Banishment less dreadful than the residing in their native Countrys.[11]

Praise be to Heaven that there have been 60 Years without Civil War or Pestilence in England and 16 without any foreign War that could deserve that name therefore Politically speaking an evacuation is necessary not only for the people but for the Government also. As Sir Walter Raleigh fully proves who says "Where many younger Sons of younger Brothers have neither Lands nor means to uphold themselves & where many Men of Trade or useful profession know not how to bestow themselves for lack of employment there can it not be avoided but that the whole Body of the State (howsoever otherwise healthfully disposed [)] should suffer anguish by the grievance of these ill affected Members.

"It sufficeth not that the Country hath wherewith to sustain even more than lives upon it, if means be wanting whereby to drive convenient participation of the general Store into a great number of well Deservers.

"In such cases there will be complaining commiseration & finally murmure (as Men are apt to lay the blame of those Evils whereof they know not the ground upon publick mismanagement[ )]."[12]

Besides the honest and unfortunate there is another species the idle poor the disposing of whom may be considered not only as a Charity to them but a benefit to our selves, since it is the removing of so many Enemys to the publick tranquility. These may be divided into Convicts and Vagrants: it is already provided that the former shall be transported at the publick expence, but the severe Laws against Vagrants are of little or no effect, for when they are put in execution which rarely happens their effect is quite different from their Design. He who is committed to Bridewell is not reformed but initiated in all the secrets of Roguery and comes out ten times wickeder than before.

It is a reflection both upon the Charity and Policy of a Christian City to see numbers of Boys healthy and strong idling about the Streets breeding up Recruits for the Street Robbers. The putting them and such Persons as have no legal Settlements into a method of earning their Bread, the rescuing them from Vice, Necessity and Idleness and training them up to labour would be a real Charity.[13]

As there are numbers of poor in England [*who are*] of little or no use [*to themselves and of little*] to the publick, there are other parts of the World where Men are as much wanting as Lands are here, places in which fertile Tracts of Land are of no value because there is none to cultivate them. Amongst the rest, [a] great part of Carolina is in this condition.

All Carolina may be divided into 3 parts, of which one is uninhabited, the other is possessed by the Indians as the third is by the English and called the Settlement. The last are only established in those places which are convenient for Water Carriage, that is to say here and there along the Sea Coast, and in few places above 60

Miles up the Rivers. The Settlement is bounded on the North by Clarendon River, and on the South by [*the South Edistow*] Port Royal River, the uninhabited part is from [*the South Edistow*] Port Royal to the Alatamaha and the Indians possess [*-ed of the*] the Lands to the West of the Settlement.[14] This Province is bounded on the North by Virginia, on the South West by the Spanish Florida, on the East and South East by the Atlantick Ocean along which it extends it self from 36 to 29 Degrees North Latitude and Westward into the Country as far as the South Seas. Described in

this manner it was granted by King Charles the second to Lord Shaftsbury and other Lord Proprietors. It was then one great Forrest thinly inhabited by small Indian Nations. About the Year 1670 some English Familys were transported thither and Colonel Sayle was appointed Governor. Afterwards it was divided into 2 Provinces North and South and notwithstanding numberless discouragements increased in People.

In North Carolina the people on their first establishment for their present conveniency dispersed themselves into Country Plantations so that there is no Town of any consideration and very little Trade there.

In South Carolina the first Planters established themselves in a Body pursuant to the Directions of Lord Shaftsbury. There is a considerable Trade and one beautiful Town consisting of about a thousand white People. This Province is watered by several noble Rivers. The first to the Northward and by which it is seperated from North Carolina is Clarendon River; about . . . Miles to the South West of Clarendon River the Sante falls into the Sea, a

River of long course which rises in the Apalachy or Cherichee Mountains. Several French Protestant Familys when forced from France by Persecution in 1686 settled here, in a forlorn condition. God has blessed their industry and they and their familys are now Masters of handsome Houses, large Tracts of cultivated Land and

numerous Herds of Cattle. At about . . . Miles to the South West
of the Sante the two Rivers of Ashly and Cooper joining each
other meet the Ocean, upon the point of Land formed by their
conflux stands Charles Town the capital of South Carolina. At
about . . . Miles from their Mouths the River Stono discharges it
self. . . . Miles farther to the North West the North Edistow
River meets the Sea; at about . . . Miles farther the South Edistow a deep and wide River falls into the Sea.[15] From the Edistow
at about . . . Miles South West along the Coast lye the Islands of
Beaufort and St. Hellens on which is a small Town from the adjoining Harbour called Port Royal looked upon to be the best for
Men of War in all Carolina. Thus far is inhabited by Europeans
and is commonly called the Settlement the strength of which
amounts to 2,500 white Men able to bear Arms and near upon
40,000 Negroes their Slaves.

The Settlement which is all the cultivated part of South Carolina bears a very small proportion to the waste part of the
Province, yet from this small spot of Land which in the year 1670
was only Woods at an averidge for some years last past hath been
imported . . . Barrells of Rice . . . Barrels of Pitch and Tarr per
Annum and some small quantitys of Silk: the latter produce hath
been very much neglected partly for the want of knowing how to
wind the Silk, partly through want of white hands, the Negroe
Slaves being both dull and careless and not capable of winding it
with that nicety which it requires. Wine also has been tried by
way of curiosity and succeeded but the Indian Massacre and unhappy division between the Proprietors and People occasioned
that and all other improvements to be neglected.[16]

To give a better idea of the place, take in his own Words Mr.
Archdales description of South Carolina [(of which this Province is
part)], a Man of undoubted veracity and Virtue, and who was for
many years Governor thereof.

" 'Tis beautified with odoriferous Woods green all the year, as Pine, Cedar & Cypress. 'Tis naturally fertile & easy to manure. Were the Inhabitants industrous Riches would flow in upon them; for I am satisfied a Person with 500£ discreetly laid out in England & again prudently managed in Carolina shall in a few years live in as much plenty as a Man of 300£ a Year in England; & if he continues careful, not covetous shall increase to great Riches, as many there are already Witnesses & many more might have been if Luxury & Intemperance had not ended their Days.

"As to the Air 'tis always serene & agreeable to any Constitutions, as the first Planters experienced. There's seldom any raging Sickness but what is brought from the Southern Colonys; as the late Sickness was, which raged A.D. 1706 & carried off abundance of People in Charles Town & other places.

"Intemperance also has occasioned some Distempers. What may properly be said to belong to the Country is to have some gentle touches of Agues & Feavers in July & August, especially to new Comers. It has a Winters Season to beget a new Spring. I was there at twice five years & had no Sickness but what I got by a careless violent cold; & indeed I perceived that the Feavers & Agues were generally gotten by carelessness in Cloathing or Intemperance.

"Every thing generally grows there that will grow in any part of Europe there being already many sorts of Fruits as Apples, Pears, Apricocks, Nectarines &c.ª They that once taste of them will despise the watry washy taste of those in England. There's such plenty of them that they are given to the Hoggs. In 4 or 5 Years they come from a Stone to be bearing Trees.

"All sorts of Grain thrive in Carolina as Wheat, Barley Pease &c.ª And I have measured some Wheat Ears 7 or 8 of our Inches long. It produces the best Rice in the known World, which is a good Commodity for returns home; as is also Pitch, Tarr, Buck,

Doe, Bears Skin & Furrs, tho' the last is not so good as the Northern Colonys.

"It has already such plenty of provisions that it in a great measure furnishes Barbadoes, Jamaica &ca There are vast numbers of wild Ducks, Geese, Teal; & the Sea & Rivers abound in Fish. That which makes Provisions so cheap is the shortness of the Winter: for having no need to mow for Winter Fodder, they can apply their hands in raising other Commoditys.

"The Rivers are found to be more Navigable than was at first believed & 'twas then prudently contrived not to settle on the most Navigable; but on Ashley & Cooper River; those entrances are not so bold as the others: So that Enemys & Pirates have been disheartened in their Designs to disturb that Settlem!

"The new Settlers have now great advantages over the first Planters, since they can be supplied with Stocks of Cattle & Corn at reasonable rates."[17]

["*We shall conclude this Account of Carolina with an Extract of a Letter from thence from a Person of credit who speaks of the Southward near the Savanah.*

"*The many Lakes we have up & down breed a multitude of Geese & other Water Fowl. All along Port Royal River & in all this part of Carolina, the Air is so temperate & the Seasons of the year so regular that there's no excess of heat or cold nor any troublesome variety of Weather: for tho' there is every year a kind of Winter, yet it is both shorter & milder than at Ashley & Cooper River, & passes over insensibly as if there was no Winter at all. This sweet temperature of Air causes the Banks of this River to be covered with various kinds of lovely Trees; which being perpetually green present a thousand Landskips to the Eye, so fine & so diversified that the sight is entirely charmed with them. The Ground is very low in most places near the River; but rises gradually at a distance with little Hills adjoining to fruitful Plains all covered with Flowers without so much as a Tree to interrupt the prospect. Beyond these are beautiful Valleys, cloathed with green Herbs & a continual verdure caused by the refreshing Rivulets that run thro' them: There are a great many Thickets which produce abundance of Simples, the Indians make use of them for the cure of their Diseases. There are also Sarsaparilla, Cassia Trees, Gums & Rossin very good for Wounds & Bruises; & such a prodigious quantity of Honey which the Bees make every where that the store of it is not to be exhausted. Of this they make excellent Spirits & Mead as good as Malaga Sack. The Bees swarm 5 or 6 times. Theres a kind of Tree from which there runs an Oil of extraordinary virtue for curing Wounds & another Tree which yields a Balm thought to be scarce inferior to that of Mecca."*][18]

[*Beyond South Edistow the Continent is at present all desolate. There a Nation of Indians called Yamasees formerly dwelt amongst whom the English lived dispersed in single Familys without so much as fortifying their Houses, but in the year 1715 the Indians destroyed all the unfortified Settlements. The terror of which incursion has prevented the inhabiting any of the Lands on the Continent to the Southward of the Edistow notwithstanding the Yamasees and other Indian Nations being almost destroyed in the Wars have retired several hundred Miles into the Country and left the Land uninhabited.*]

From the River of Port Royal to the south is the uninhabited Carolina part of which his Majesty has Erected into a new Province by the name of Georgia in this past Act.[19] At . . . Miles distance from [*South Edistow*] Port Royal, one of the mouths of the Savanah opens into the Ocean, it rises in the Cherichee Mountains and after forming several Lakes washes the place where the Savanah Town formerly stood,[20] thence with an easy Stream runs through a flat Countrey and after a course of near 600 Miles from its Fountains falls into the Sea through several mouths. At a Days sail to the Southward of the mouths of the Savanah the Alatamaha mixes with the Ocean and forms a number of beautiful Islands. Up this River at a place called the Forks of Alatamaha, there was a little Fort and English Garrison of regular Troops.[21]

The Countreys lying between the Savanah and Alatamaha which are granted by his Majesty to this [*Charity*] Trust are little known to the English they never having extended their Plantations so far. All the printed Maps are false, yet have we had a description of them from Men of undoubted credit, some of whom traversed that Country in hunting, some on Messages to the Indians and one Gentleman out of Philosophical curiosity descended the Savanah for several hundred Miles, in order to observe the various natural productions of that Country of which he is now in a most beautiful Book publishing an Account.[22]

This Tract of Land lyes in the same Latitude with Schiras in Persia and Jerusalem in Palestine. The Climate is hot in Summer but the heat is much abated and the Air cooled by North West Winds and runing Streams. The Winters are short and the Frosts though not severe are sufficient to kill the Insects and purify the Air. Many Rivers and Brooks fall into the Sea between the Savanah and Alatamaha. The Sea Coast is guarded from the rage of the Atlantick Ocean by a range of Islands most of which are adorned with lofty Woods intermixed with Savannas, that is to say Meadows which are naturally clear of Trees. The Channels between the Islands and the Continent are safe from all Weather. The Sea Coast of the Continent is level and without any considerable Hills. The Soil is for the most part of a fertile Land, in some places of a more barren kind, the whole Shore is covered with Wood, that which is most fertile bearing black Wallnut Trees, Hiccory, Cedar, Cypress and Mulberry Trees: the more barren is covered with Oak, Firr and Pine Trees, and the richness or barreness of the Soil is as well distinguished by the species as by the growth of the Timber. From the Sea Coast up into the Country to where the Hills begin the Land rises gently with what the Gardeners call a hanging level Excepting in some small hills which run across the Country and Jetting into the rivers from bluff Points.[23] All the way are Woods intermixed with Savannas and

watered with small Streams, which when stopped by the fall of
rotten Trees or other impediment form what in that Countrey
they call Swamps or Marshes made by runing Water, in them
grow Canes and Reeds the young Shoots and Leaves of which are
green in the most scorching Summers and [*are the food of*] feed
innumerable herds of Deer and wild Cattle [*with which those woods
abound*]. The Woods are for the most part composed of tall
Trees, which intermingling their branches form such a shade as
prevents any Shrubs, Briers or Underwoods growing underneath
them, the Vine only excepted which mounting up the Trees to
their tops enjoys the Sun. As the Trees are large, stand at great
distances and extend their Boughs far, the Woods are in the most
places [*passage*] passable for Horsemen. At about 90 Miles from
the Sea in some places and 150 in others the Country rises into
little Hillocks, the Lands are richer the Trees still larger: as it
extends Westwards the Hills increase in height: at about 400
Miles distance they rise into Mountains and in the Valleys formed
by them, Wood, Lakes, Savannas intermixed with Rocks [*of Mar-
ble*] and falls of Water form beautiful Landskips. Beyond these
Mountains we cannot find that any English have ever yet been.

[*It appears that*] In short all the Land between the Rivers Savanah and Alatamaha is at present a Forrest diver[s]ified with
Groves, Lawns, Swamps, Rivers, Lakes and Mountains abounding
with Staggs, Elks, Buffaloes, wild Horses, black Cattle and numberless other kind of Creatures, besides which these vast Woods
shelter Beasts of Prey, Serpents and other venomous Insects.

Towns for Trade might be conveniently situated along the
sides of the Navigable Rivers. For the subsistance and employment of the Inhabitants of each Town there might be alotted
a particular Produce peculiar to that place, natural to that Climate
and such as England is now obliged to buy from Foreigners. The
Timber being felled the Ground it grew on would become arable,
the Swamps being drained would become Meadow and by the

clearing of the Woods the noxious Animals would retire or be destroyed. Villages and Farms might be established in the Lands farther from the Rivers and the most distant from Water Carriage would be convenient for breeding and grazing of Cattle. The Woods growing upon barren Lands or such as are not fit for cultivation might be preserved for the benefit of future Generations. Every part of the Country will produce Wheat, Barley, Indian Corn; Fruits of all kinds as Peaches, Pears etc. and all sorts of Cattle known in Europe, as Horses, Oxen etc.

Some Towns besides the provisions of Corn and Cattle may raise Hemp and Flax and considering that they [are] will be free from the burthens of Superstition, Taxes and high Rents which the Countrys from whence those [Produces] Commoditys are brought groan under and considering the fertility of Soils never yet broke up, it is to be believed that they may furnish Flax and Hemp much cheaper than any of the Continents of Europe can. Other Towns may be employed on raising Vines and Mulberry Trees for the Silk Worms. Where the Soyl is more proper for it Olive Yards may be the support of the adjoining Town. Various other Productions will maintain various Towns and the exchanging of them for English Commoditys or for each other will create an intercourse and traffick.

The Lands near the Sea will produce Flax, Hemp, Mulberry Trees for the Silk Worms; Cotton, Indico. Olives, Dates, Raisins, Pitch, Tarr and Rice the two last of which are needless, there being enough of them produced in the present Settlement.

Higher up the Rivers and in Hilly Countrys good Wine might be made and perhaps the Mohair Goat might keep the fineness of its Fleece there as well as in Angria. Gums, Barks and Woods fit for dying all kinds of Colours might be also there raised [and indeed every kind of Produce with which England is now supplied from Countrys lying in the same Latitude].

The taking the method of Agriculture from Countrys lying near

21

Commoditys appropriated to each town

What Lands near the Sea will Produce

What the Land up the Country will produce

the same Climate and of a like Soyl and the having Men from those Countrys to instruct the first Planters may not be improper. A Native of Piedemont an intelligent Man who is lately come from South Carolina says That the Soyl and Air resemble Lombardy only the first is richer the latter hotter than in that part of Italy and that the same manner of Cultivation may be followed.[24] That the Mulberry Trees may be planted at equal distances Vines may be reared against them and Wheat sowed between, that the shaddow of the Trees may defend the Corn and Grapes from the too scorching heats of the Sun, that the Leaves may be gathered by the Women and Children to feed the Silk Worms. [*This method of Agriculture will be more fully mentioned in another Treatise.*][25]

This Tract of Land not only wants People for the cultivation of it but also for the preservation of South Carolina. From the settling of that Colony till after Mr. Archdale was Governor who did strict Justice to the Indians the English and they lived intermixed like People of the same Nation. Afterwards some of the English in South Carolina who are known by the name of Indian Traders and travel from Nation to Nation furnishing the Indians with European Goods, taking from them in exchange Skins and other Commoditys injured the Natives by extortion and violencys committed upon their Wives. They demanded redress, which not being procured, by one sudden irruption they almost destroyed the whole Plantation. The English had carelessly dispersed themselves in single Familys through the Country as if it had been entirely subjected relying wholly upon the Indian faith and at the same time injured and refused justice to those brave, well armed and revengeful Nations upon whose Faith they relied.

In the year 1715 it was that the Yamasee Indians having called to their aid a large body of other Nations from beyond the Savanah River, destroyed all the English unfortified Houses to within 5 Miles of Charles Town. Those who had caution enough to fortify their Settlements escaped the Storm in which many hundred familys of negligent Planters perished. The War thus begun continued to the great expence and almost entire ruin of the Colony, and at last was ended by an universal Peace, the Yamasees who scorned submission having abandoned their Lands and all the other Indian Nations having retired either beyond the Alatamaha or into the Mountains. Notwithstanding the Peace the terror of the Massacre remains so strongly imprinted upon the people of South Carolina that they dare not attempt in single Familys to settle beyond the River [*Edistow*] of Port Royal and have not a number of white Inhabitants sufficient to make Settlements in a Body.

The District intended for a new Colony whilst it lyes uninhabited will facilitate the Invasions of the Indians upon South Carolina. But a number of Towns established along the Rivers Savanah and Alatamaha would prevent any future Massacre and make a stronger Barrier to the present Settlement and keep the Negroe Slaves of South Carolina in awe who are now so numerous as to be dreadul even to their Masters.[26]

It is surprizing to think that notwithstanding in America there are fertile Lands sufficient to subsist all the useless poor in England and distresst Protestants in Europe, yet that thousands should starve here for want of meer sustenance: but the reason is the distance makes it very difficult for them to go thither. The same want that renders Men useless here prevents their paying their Passage, and if others pay it for them they become Servants or rather Slaves for years to those who have defrayed that charge. Therefore Money for Passage is necessary, but it is not the only want: for if the people were set down in America and the Land before them; they must cut down Trees, build Houses, fortify Towns and dig and sow the Land before they can get in a Harvest, and till then they must be provided with Food and kept together that they may be assistant to each other in the support and protection of the whole.

The sending forth of Colonys the Romans esteemed amongst their noblest works for which they appointed Officers who directed the management of the whole and the expence was bore out of the publick Treasury.[27] And his Majesty for deducing Colonys into America hath incorporated Trustees with the Powers of the Roman Officers, they therefore are to gather such People as are proper to be sent over and to take care that they shall be there established in a regular manner. Of which Machival gives his opinion as follows. . . .[28]

The Trustees intend to make experiment of all kind of Products as silk wine oil etc. etc. divulge the manner of rearing them that all the American planters may Proffit by them and be there by enabled to buy more English Manufactures.[29]

The Gentlemen who compose this Society have restrained themselves in their Charter from receiving any benefit by the Design. To the carrying on of [the Charity] which they give not only their time but also Benefactions in Money, and are permitted to choose into the Trust any whom they shall find inclined and capable to be assisting in so humane and Christian an undertaking. They rely for success first upon that providence which supports Mankind, next upon the charitable disposition of the people of England, and they doubt not that much will be spared from Luxury and superfluous expences by generous tempers when a means is offered them by the giving of [10] 20 Pounds to provide for a Man or Woman or by [5] 10 Pounds a Child forever. Many Persons of distinguished Characters have honoured the Trust so far as to be Patrons and accept of Powers for collecting of Benefactions, Lists of whom are hereunto annexed.[30]

In order to prevent the [*Charity*] benefactions given to this purpose from ever being misapplied, and to keep up as far as human precaution can the Spirit of disinterestedness they have established the following method of accounting. First, That all their transactions may appear and that each Benefactor may see what Money has been laid out and what remains All Monies given, shall be as soon as received by the Cashier of the Trustees deposited in the Bank of England and inserted in printed Lists with the Names of the Benefactors, or if concealed, then the Names of those by whose hands they sent their Money. Secondly there shall be Annual Accounts laid before the Lord high Chancellor, the Master of the Rolls, two chief Justices, Chief Baron of the Exchequer or any two of them; and printed Coppys of the said Accounts shall be transmitted to every Benefactor who hath given above the Sum of 5 Pounds Annual Benefaction or above 100 Pounds in one Sum. These Accounts will show the Money that hath been laid out and the printed Lists the Money that hath been received, and in this Account will be contained the numbers, names and ages of the persons sent abroad, the Charges of Passage, Cloaths, Arms etc. and also the amount of all profits that shall from time to time arise from the Colony, which will in one view give the state of the affairs of the Trust.[31]

And for the continuation of the [*Charity*] Trust there will be labour and Lands reserved in America: So that at the same time the Money by being laid out preserves the lives of the poor and makes a comfortable provision for them whose expences are by it defrayed, their labour in improving their own Lands will make the adjoining reserved Lands valuable and the Rents of those reserved Lands will be a perpetual Fund for the relieving more poor people. So that instead of laying out the Money upon Lands with the income thereof to support the poor, this is laying [*out the Charity*] it out upon the poor and by the relieving those who are now unfortunate raises a Fund for the perpetual relief of those who shall be so hereafter.[32]

The Trustees must consider of the manner of executing this trust and may take in Proposals accept and Inquire.[33] The first Colony must be composed of People able to bear fatigue, they being established the weaker and more helpless poor may be sent over, and how even they may be made capable of subsisting themselves and be beneficial to the publick will be shown [*hereafter*] on another occasion.[34]

In chusing the first [*Colony*] Famelyes regard should be had to the preventing those Evils by which infant Colonys have frequently been destroyed. The English attempts in America have often miscarried by Disertion, Sickness, Famine, Mutiny or force of an Enemy, as did the late glorious but unsuccessful attempt of his Grace the Duke of Montague.[35]

The first Colony should consist not of single Men but of Familys: for a Wife and Children are security for a Mans not abandoning the Settlement; and the presence of those dear pledges who will reap the advantage of it will the more strongly incite him to labour. Even in the beginning Women and Children will not be useless Mouths since there will always be some business which they may do and save so much labour to the Men, such as preparing their Food, cleaning and mending their Cloaths, gathering Wild Fruits, Roots, or Shell fish etc.

The being kept clean and having wholesome food prepared at regular hours would tend greatly to the preserving the health of the people; and in Sickness the having their Wives to nurse them may recover many who would inevitably perish were they to have no succour but from careless or unskilful Comrades.

The familys should be laborious and honest people whose motive for leaving their Country should not be Crimes but Misfortunes. Their industry and labour employed in cultivating the

Land being helped by one year provision will be a remedy against Famine.

They ought to be apprized of the nature of the Design and the difficultys they must at first undergo and none taken but who after pious consideration are sensible of the advantages they will reap by having Houses and Lands of their own sufficient to give a comfortable maintenance to themselves and familys for ever. Without doubt such Men would not be apt to mutiny, since that would be destroying the end they aim at. If the number of Men able to bear Arms be sufficient to make head against the first attempts of any Enemy that can be drawn together in that Country it will be sufficient to protect them from open force.

The manner of collecting them may be first by publishing Proposals of the terms they are to go upon, in some such manner as this.

This is to give notice that all Persons whose necessitys render them desireous of reaping the benefit of the intended Colony, may send in Writing their Names, place of abode at present and for 3 years last past, what Trades or Occupations they understand, their own ages and if they are married the ages of their Wives and number and ages of their Children, to the Secretary of the Trustees, and after 10 Days in which their Characters shall be enquired into, if the Trustees find them to their satisfaction they will be admitted of the Colony with the following advantages.

They will be subsisted till the Ships are ready to sail at the *1st* House belonging to the Trustees, where they will have an allowance of salt-Provisions in order to accustom them to what they are to meet with at Sea.

On their being imbarked they, their Wives and Children are to *2dly* be Cloathed from head to foot at the expence of the Society.

They are to have Bedding and Hamocks sufficient for them- *3dly* selves and familys given unto each of them.

4thly	Each family is to have Kitchen Utensils, working Tools,[36] Seed and other necessarys given gratis on their landing. Each person who hath an Apprentice will be allowed to take him with him provided the same is above 14 and under 20 years of age.
5thly	Each family is to have provisions for one Year.
	In return of all these benefits and for the preservation of themselves and of the Colony they are to conform to the following Regulations.
1st	They are to be obedient to their Directors.
2dly	They are to assist each other and by joint endeavours fortify such place as their chief Commander shall think proper to establish their Town in.
3dly	They are by joint indeavours to build Houses for themselves and cultivate and sow Lands for their next years provision.
4thly	After that is done, the Houses that are built and the Land that is cultivated are to be divided amongst themselves, each Man to have a House and 20 Acres of Land to himself and to his Heirs Male forever, to be held in Coppyhold at Fine certain. In lieu of which fine and Rent each Man is to pay for his House and Land, one Days labour in the Week, which labour is to be employed in the service of the publick.
5thly	All Persons that have 3 Children alive at the same time, shall during the time of their 3 Childrens being alive at once be exempted from the Rent of labour.
6thly	All Persons above 60 years of age shall be exempt from labour.
7thly	No Person shall leave the Country in two years without license obtained, which shall not be refused any one who will repay to the Commander in chief the expence which the Trustees have been at on his Account.
8thly	All Persons that go are themselves and familys to be free and no labour, taxes, tythes nor Money under any pretence whatsoever is to be exacted from them, save only the above mentioned Labour,

which is to be the Rent for their Lands, the produce of which labour is to be laid out for the support of the Colony in time of War, Sickness or Famine and for the sending over more poor Familys to increase it.[37]

Lastly, all the Males from 17 years of age to 45 shall be obliged to take up Arms in defence of the Colony, and shall be exercised for that purpose.

Of the Persons who shall give in their Names to the Secretary, the Trustees will chuse such as are sober, healthy and able to labour, whose Familys are not too numerous in young Children and provide a House to subsist them in till they can be imbarked, where they may be accustomed to that Discipline which they are to preserve when abroad. Those who are impatient of orderly Government may be dismissed and the Wheat whinnowed from the Chaff, for it is infinitely better to lose expence some Weeks than to carry over a mutinous or effeminate fellow.

When the number of people for the intended Colony are chosen they may be divided into hundreds of familys, a proper person is to be appointed Constable over each hundred, the hundred is to be divided into Laths consisting of 25 Men and their Familys. Out of them one is to be Constable and the other 24 to be divided into two Tythings, out of each of which a Tything Man is to be appointed, the Tythings to be subdivided into Comradeships of 6 one of whom is to be Foreman. The Man is to be answerable for the behaviour of his Wife, Children and Servants, and to enable him to keep them in order he is to have proper authority over them, the Foreman is to be answerable for his Comrades to the Tything Man, and he to the Constable for his Tything, the Constable is to be accountable for his Lath to the Constable of the hundred.[38]

Under the ancient simple English Laws, our Saxon Ancestors from small beginings grew into a mighty Nation, those Laws were calculated for Warlike and tumultuous times, a hardy race of Men in a woody and thinly peopled Country exposed to the frequent ravages of unexpected Enemys. Notwithstanding all these inconveniencys, that great Prince King Aelfrid by dividing England into Hundreds secured the publick Peace so well that an unarmed Man loaded with Gold might safely have travelled from one end of England to the other. As England in that age was in the same condition as Georgia is now, the same Laws will probably have the same effect and the binding the Officers and Inhabitants of the Tythings and Hundreds to produce the Offenders or be answerable for the Offence may as effectually now preserve the publick tranquility in Georgia as it did then in England.

It may not perhaps be improper for incouragement of Virtue and Industry to establish two other Degrees, that is to say Yeomenry and Gentry. That such of the Townsmen as shall signalize themselves by their Sobriety, Diligence and Capacity in Agriculture, Mechanicks or any other useful knowledge may be advanced according to their merit. Into the Yeomenry also may be admitted such Persons as shall carry over their familys at their own expence and agree with the Trustees on such terms as shall be for the advantage of the Colony.

The Gentry are to be Men of Reputation and Character and such to whom the Trustees shall think fit for the increase of the Colony to grant Manors upon such terms as shall be agreed between them, which Agreement shall be specified in the Grants unto them and be inrolled in their Courts. All the benefits arising from such Agreements are to be employed in supporting the Colony.

The Election being carefully looked to which is a matter of the highest importance, since if the first men have not Bodys and Minds capable for the undertaking, it would be as vain to attempt a Settlement as it would be for a Carpenter to work without

Tools; the next thing is the imbarkation on which they should have their new Cloaths and Beding delivered unto them and be reviewed by such of the Trustees and Benefactors as are willing to see the fruits of their Charity. For preserving them in their Passage it will be necessary that the Ship should not be crouded, that they should be brought up frequently on Deck for the benefit of the fresh Air and that in the mean time the places where they lye should be washed with Vinegar and proper things burnt therein to take away all nauseous smells, cleanliness being of great consequence to health, whilst the Men might be taught the use of the Musket. These things belong to the Leader of the Colony to execute and he must be one who will look upon the Colony as his Family, upon the preserving of individuals depend both his Reputation and the success of the Settlement.

For the inducing the people to the more easy obedience it may be proper that he should give those who are most orderly and virtuous some extraordinary allowance of refreshments and to punish those who behave in a contrary manner. But if the Crimes be such as require severe punishments then they ought to be tried before a Court of Judicature composed in such manner as the Society shall appoint. The utmost endeavours should be used to instill a spirit of labour into the poor People, for extream necessity generally breaks the minds of the distressed and throws them into a habit of idleness very difficult to be cured. For the remedying of this ill habit the method would be that such of the poor as seem most industrious should be encouraged and that out of them should be appointed Tything Men and Foremen. The Constables ought to be Men that should understand the nature of the Climate to which the Colony is to be sent and to know those Arts which are necessary for the first Establishment. They should instruct the Tything-Men and Fore-Men in those things which are most necessary to be done at their landing, they should acquaint them with the nature of building Houses, clearing Woods, mending and making their own Tools and also the Seasons and manner of Diging, Plowing and Sowing of Corn etc. raising Provisions and managing Hemp, Silk, Vines etc.

By often conversing of these matters in the Voyage the People will grow eager to arrive in Port in order to put them in practice. The Women should be inspired with the same Spirit of labour, such as understand making of Cloaths, Spining of Linnen etc. and household services should be encouraged, so as to make others emulate them and be allowed something for instructing those who are ignorant: little prizes for those who are most expert may be perhaps a good way of incouraging industry both in Men and Women.

Great care ought to be taken in instructing them in their Duty towards God and Man; and a wise Minister might take many occasions to urge such Precepts home when their minds were most inclined to receive them from Storms and other accidents which frequently happen on the face of the deep. It would be highly proper that the Minister should assemble those who are of the Church of England Evening and Morning and that those who are of other perswasions should frequently assemble themselves to praise God in their way. All kind of refreshments should be on board for relief of the Sick, and the same care ought to be taken of the poorest Colonian, if any of them should be afflicted with Sickness as of the principal Officer.

After their arrival, in establishing the Town regard must be had to preserving the Inhabitants from Sickness, from foreign Enemys and civil discord: the last will depend upon the Laws, the other two in great measure upon the situation of the place As will also their future subsistance since they must owe their maintenance to the fertility of the Soil for raising and convenience of carriage for exporting their production, and therefore the nature of the place ought to be well inquired into.

The Ancients were very curious in choosing situations for Citys; and the regular founding of them having been an Art long neglected, it may not be improper to hear Vitruvius Engineer to C. Julius Caesar on that Account.[39]

"Before the Walls are begun to be built it is fit to choose a healthy situation. Such are rising Grounds or little Hills in an Air not thick nor subject to Foggs & the descent facing those points of the Compass which in that Climate are least exposed to the heats or colds: It ought not to be near Marshes: for when the Morning Breezes which rise before the Sun shall bear towards the Town, the Vapours rising from the stinking Mud mixed with the breaths of Cattle infected with feeding in fenny Pastures, the Bodys of the Townmen will be liable to many Distempers from the unwholesomeness of the Morning Air. Situations upon the Sea shore exposed to the South or West are seldom healthy, because during the Summer the Sun from its rising begins to heat & at Noon Day burns the Southern expositions. The Western ones are warmed by the rising, heated by the mid-Day & scorched before the setting Sun: & by the great change from the colds of the Night to the violent heats of the Day, the health of the Inhabitants of those are greatly prejudiced: & this may be observed in inanimate things, for in Vaults where one would keep Wine no body lets in the light on the Western or Southern sides but on the Northern only, because that exposition is never subject to change from heat to cold. It is remarked that the Store-houses open to the Sunny side keep neither Corn, Fruits nor Provisions well: for the Sun drying up those parts in which the strength of their natural virtue consists, makes them moulder & consume.———If any one desires to search curiously into the situations of Citys I should advise him to observe the nature of the Fish, Fowl & Beasts feeding on that place. In doing which he will find great difference in their temperature, according to the healthiness or unhealthiness of the place.———Certainly we ought to choose the most temperate situation if we would have the City healthy. If we inquire the reason why the Ancients sacrificed & inspected the Entrails of Beasts which fed in the places where they intended to erect Citys, we shall find if their Entrails were corrupted they sacrificed others, that they might the better judge whether it arose from the Sickness of that particular Beast or the fault of the Pasture: if they on repeated experiments found the Beasts healthy & their Entrails fair & sound they concluded the Water & the Herbage healthy, & there fixed their habitations: but if they found them decayed & rotten they never fixed in that situation, judging that human Bodys would be affected by the unwholesomeness of the Water & Pastures by which the Beasts on whom they were to be subsisted were nourished.———If the Town be built amongst Morasses & that they lye along the Coast facing the North or North East, if these Fens should be higher than the Beech, the City may be healthfully situated: for it is but opening Ditches & whenever the Sea is swelled by Storms it will flow in, & the salt-Waters intermixing with the Waters of the Morass will prevent them from corrupting & will kill any unwholesome Insects bred in them. This is demonstrated by the Marshes of Gaul, particularly about Ravenna & Aquilea, which Citys tho' surrounded with Fenns are very healthy. On the other hand where the Waters are standing & can have no Ditches or Drains to draw them into the Rivers or Sea, they corrupt, stink & send up pestilential vapours very dangerous to the health of the neighbour^{ng} Inhabitants. Such was those in Apulia adjoining to the ancient Salapia, a Town built by Diomedes after his return from Troy. The Inhabitants were every year afflicted with epidemical Distempers. They in the Reign of Marcus Hostilius prayed him to point them out a healthy place to which they might remove & build a City. That gracious Prince having with great care searched out, at last found a healthy situation on the Sea Coast, & having asked & obtained the consent of the people & Senate of Rome to transplant the City of Salapia thither, he marked out the Walls, divided the City into equal Portions for the Inhabitants whom he taxed half a Sester a head, he dug Trenches from an adjoining Lake to the Sea, he made that the Port for the Town. So that the Salapians being remov'd only 4 Miles from their ancient habitations lived now in a healthy, regular & well laid out City.

"Having taken care that the situation should be healthy, it is to be wished that the adjoining Country may be fertile & abound with Provisions. The high Roads ought to be convenient, & the City should be near either to a Sea Port or a Navigable River for the convenience of Water Carriage.———It is also necessary that the Streets should be so disposed as to be sheltered from the coldest, the hotest & the moistest Winds, the excess of which qualitys are greatly hurtful to human Bodys. This was neglected by the Founders of Mitylene a City in the Isle of Lesbos famous for magnificent buildings, but so inconsideratedly laid out, that when the West Winds blow feavers, when Corus the Asthma rages, & tho' when the Wind changes to the North the Town grows healthy, yet the severity of the cold is then such that there is no staying in the Streets nor Squares———If the Streets are sheltered from these Winds, it not only preserves the health of those that are well, but contributes greatly to the recovering the Sick who labour under such Distempers as are affected by the Air, as Dizziness, Coughs, Plurecy, Ptisick, spitting of blood & such kind of Distempers as are not cured by evacuations but by restoratives & nutrition. These Distempers generally caused by cold, (the strength of the Pat[i]ent being already wore out with his Distempers) are very hard to cure. In these Cases an Air agitated by violent Winds is very prejudicial; but on the contrary a mild & calm Air sheltered from the rages of the Winds & not impregnated with too many cold or moist particles contributes greatly to restore the Patients extenuated with long Sickness, swells their Vessels & prepares them for Nutrition."

The Roman Architect directs to consult the wholesomeness of the Air and Waters, fertility of the Soil, the convenience of Navigation and easy access: He gives many Rules by which to judge of them, for the Design of his whole work is to teach how to build a strong convenient and magnificent City.

The situation of the Town being fixed upon, it ought first to be fortified in such a manner as may make it defensible against the insults of any Enemy that can attack it in that distant quarter of the World. This ought to take place of all other cares and herein the example of the wise Athenians may be followed. Who "After the defeat of the Persians at Platea returned home, & tho' the most part of their Houses at Athens were burnt or broken down, yet they resolv'd first on their common defence & to fortify their City before they cared to cover themselves, their Wives & Children with any private Buildings."[40] A Ditch well flanked and Pallisadoed will very probably be a sufficient Fortification, which in a short space of time may be finished. At the same time that one Detatchment of Men are cutting the Trees, digging the Ditch, fixing the Pallisadoes and mounting of Cannon, another Detatchment may be running up the private and publick Buildings, which at first for expeditions sake will be of Boards, and two Carpenters considering the Timber grows upon the place may build a wooden House in a few Days. In the distribution of the Town the Streets should be spacious and laid out by Line and a large Square reserved for a Market place, and for exercising the Inhabitants, on the sides of which may be the Church, Infirmary for the Sick, an House for new Comers, Town House and other publick Buildings. Without the Town a Mile square which amounts to 640 Acres might be reserved as a Common for the pasturing of the Cattle and all within Musket shot of the Works should be cleared. This open space will contribute greatly to the health and security of the Town as well as to the conveniency of the Inhabitants. The Lands beyond the Common may be divided into Laths, each Lath to consist of 32 Farms, 6 to be reserved for the publick benefit of the Colony, 2 for the Constable and one for each Family. Each Family should have a Farm in the Country and an Alotment sufficient for a House and Garden in the Town. The Leader of the Colony should take care with the utmost expedition to have an Acre cleared and sowed upon each Farm and a House built upon each Alotment in the Town. After the Land is divided into Farms and the Town into Alotments and a House built upon each Alotment and an Acre sowed upon each Farm, it may not be improper that a Thanksgiving Day be appointed, on which the People should in their cleanest and best Apparel assemble themselves in the great Square by break of Day, and begin the Day by Prayers and Thanksgiving to God for his delivering them from misery and establishing them in a happy State of life. After Prayers the Men should stand to their Arms in the Square and the Drums beating, the Town and the Colony may be publickly named.

After the naming the Town and Province the Articles or Laws under which they are to Governed should be read and it would be proper to give a Name to each Lath. Then the 25 Men of each Lath being drawn up seperately with the Constables at the head of them, they should draw Lots for the Lands, and then the Foremen of each Comradeship should draw Lots for what Lands should belong to their Comradeships and the People should draw Lots for their Farms. After this the Cannon and small Shot may be fired and the rest of the Day spent in Manly Exercises and in decent joy and gladness a comfortable Meal being provided for the whole People at the expence of the Society and the same Day of that Month may be kept every Year as a Thanksgiving Day for the establishment of the Colony and in commemoration of the Founder, *if the Town be founded by the benefaction of a single Person.*

The Town should consist of 125 Familys since that number may have their Farms within two Miles of the Town for it will be inconvenient to go farther to their Lands therefore those who exceed that number should be divided into Laths consisting of 25 Familys. Each Lath should compose a Village which should be fortified and in it each Family should have its Alotment as also Farms thereunto adjoining in the same manner as the Towns People. And still as the People increase new Laths may be set out and new Villages built till they amount to 20 dependant on one Town. All which Villagers and Townsmen being drawn together will form a Batallion of Infantry consisting of 625 Men.

If any Persons shall signalize themselves by their merit and will bear their own expences they may as is before mentioned be called Yeomen and ought to have larger Portions of Land marked out for them beyond the Villages and to 4 Yeomen should be alotted the same quantity of Land as to one Lath. They should be obliged to build their 4 Houses together to fortify them with a Ditch to keep themselves and Servants Armed and perhaps it may not be improper that by the terms of their Agreement they should as Dragoons serve on Horseback with two Men if the Country should be invaded. Ten such Laths of Yeomenry will make 120 Dragoons. If any Gentlemen should carry over a number of Foreigners for Servants they ought to be planted beyond the Yeomenry and the same quantity of Land as is alotted for a Lath should be erected into a Manor and the service demanded for it might be besides Rent perhaps 10 Horsemen well mounted and armed. If 10 Manors should be taken up it would make 100

Horse. Between each two Laths belonging to the Yeomenry and
between each two Manors belonging to the Gentry there should
be one Lath reserved for the Colony.

If such a disposition should take place the force of each Township would consist of 625 Foot, 120 Dragoons and 100 Horse. Besides, the Lands reserved for the Charity would give room for increase for though part of them ought to be kept for Timber and felled one year under another and though some of them ought to be appropriated for the maintenance of Fortifications Artillery and Shipping yet part of them may [be] let out to such persons as do not care to be obliged to Military service and would rather pay Rent than be subject to Discipline.

The 6 Farms reserved in each Lath belonging to the Townsmen and Villagers may be cultivated by the reserved services of the Men of that Lath. The reserved service is one Day in six, therefore each Lath must furnish 4 Men every Day. The Leader of the Colony should study to make the Days of labour on the publick Land rather Days of mirth than of toil. The Workmen should be allowed Drink and Food out of the publick Stores. There Should be also pains taken to inform them that they are working for their own advantage and that the produce of those Lands is to be laid up in the Store-Houses that there may be a Magazine for supplying the Poor the Sick and the whole Town in case of War, Famine or other accidents, that by this small labour they are exempted from Taxes Tythes Rents and all other kinds of Payments and that it is but a small return to the Charity for Arming, Cloathing, Supporting and all other benefits which they have received from it.

There will be Teams kept by the Trustees and Persons appointed by them who understand the method of Agriculture used in Italy, in the Maderas and Palestine that they may cultivate the reserved Lands so as to produce Silk, Wine, Oil and other Commoditys which England is now obliged to buy at foreign Markets. Whatever is produced by these reserved Farms, after the Aged and Sick of the Laths where it grew are first provided for the remainder will be disposed of to the best advantage for the use of the Charity.

If this method can be executed in one Town the same may be repeated in any other place and a number of Towns may be planted along the Rivers Savanah and Alatamaha in the same manner. If the first 125 Familys found a Town the Villagers and Yeomenry will be drawn together by the protection of it, and therefore each 125 Familys may be settled in a seperate Town leaving the increase and the execution of the rest of the Design to time.

To defend the People from each other proper Laws will be necessary and nothing is more likely to establish unity than this equal distribution of Land and registring that distribution. There will be no room for Law Suites concerning property if the Farms are to descend undivided to the next Heir and the personal Estate be divided according to the custom of London. The only objection to this is that the younger Children will be poorly provided for. But as soon as there are 24 men who have no Land a new Village and Lath will be set out: the Daughters will be provided for by Marriage, for where Children are Wealth to their Parents and where there is more Land than People to cultivate it, no Man who is out of his Apprenticeship will remain unmarried, and as Males and Females are born in equal numbers if all the Men have Wives there can be no Woman without a Husband. The Laws will be prepared by the Trustees and assented to by the King, they will be calculated to punish all kind of violence to prevent Luxury and Oppression in the Superiors and Idleness and Vice in the Inferiors and will all have a view to the Peace and Safety of the People,[41] the promoting of Christianity and the encouragement of Commerce and Agriculture. The execution of the Laws will be in a Council of the wisest and best Men of the Colony and under them in the Constables and Tything Men as is before mentioned. But the trying of all facts relating to Criminal or Civil matters will be in Jurys of 12 Men being Peers to the Partys concerned.

As the Townships increase in number other provisions may be made and other Jurisdictions described in order to deside differences between Town and Town or the Inhabitants of different Towns.

The People of South Carolina have already promised to the Trustees that they will deliver to them on demand at Charles Town one years Provision for every Person that shall Land in the Province.[42] Besides which for fear of accidents 3 Months Provisions will be imbarked with them. So that there can be no fear of want and after their first Harvest is in they will abound in all things considering the fertility of the Soil and that Cattle thrive wonderfully there.

As for the future subsistance it must depend upon Grazing, Agriculture and raising Flax, Silk, Hemp and such kind of gross Commoditys as will be proper to keep up a Trade with and purchase from England Cloathing, Household Goods and such other things as they shall want.

To encourage Marriage and make Children a profit instead of a burthen to their Parents it may not be improper to revive the Paternal Power and give the Father the benefit of his Sons labour till he is 21 Years of age and of the Daughter's till she is married. Thus by the seven last years of his Sons labour the Father will be repaid the charge he hath been at for him from his Birth to that time. The Roman Law might be expedient exempting the Father of 3 Children from all Dutys whatsoever. Perhaps the taking up of all Vagrants in England who have no Settlements under the age of 14 Years and the binding them Apprentices to the first industrious

Planters may not be a bad method of increasing the Colony, disburthening England from future Thieves and of providing for those unhappy Wretches.

The reserved Lands being managed to the best advantage will in time produce a very considerable Revenue which is to be employed in transporting more poor Familys upon the same footing. So that the more that Revenue grows the more Towns and Villages there will be, and the more People there are the more consumption there will be of English Goods and the more Manufacturers employed. Another thing that would contribute greatly towards the support and increase of the Colony would be opening Fairs at stated times in the Commons adjoining to each Town where the Prizes of Goods should be fixed and equal justice should be done to Native or Stranger Christian or Indian and then making of Presents to the Natives and inviting them down to them will create an intercourse and traffick.

As for the benefits that will arise from Contributions given to this purpose the first will be to the Benefactors the unutterable pleasure and satisfaction which every good and generous Mind receives on its being conscious of having performed a great, a virtuous or a charitable action: and what can be a truer Charity than the giving Bread to the hungry, Cloaths to the naked, liberty of Religion to the oppressed for Conscience sake? What more human than rescuing unfortunate Youth or abandoned and helpless Orphans from the temptations want or ill Company may expose them to? What more glorious than of these to form well regulated Towns, to give them Houses, Cattle and Lands of Inheritance, to instruct them how to raise all those good things which make Life comfortable and how to enjoy them under such Laws as tend to make them happy both here and hereafter.

The relieving of the starving Wretches themselves and of their friends who are burthened with them will be but a small part of the Charity. Many Children will owe their very being to it, who would otherwise never have been born and many more their well being. The persecuted and distresst Protestants will be by this relieved, they will gain by their sufferings; instead of the Rocky Alps or the Marshes of Poland they will have the fertile Plains of Carolina, a Land of Corn, Vines and Olives, a glorious reward even in this Life for their constancy.[43]

The People of England will be greatly augmented and numberless poor will be here employed for supplying of them with necessarys. For the more People are drawn off the more room is left for others to supply their places, of which Sir Walter Rauleigh speaks very fully in the following Passage.

"And to say what I think if our King Edward the 3ᵈ had prospered in his French Wars & Peopled with English the Towns which he won as he began at Callice [Calais] driving out the French, the Kings (as his Successors) holding the same course would by this time have filled all France with our Nation without any notable emptying of this Island.

"The like may be affirmed upon like suspicion upon the French in Italy or almost of any others, as having been verified by the Saxons in England & Arabians in Barbary: what is then become of so huge a multitude as would have overspread a great part of the Continent. Surely they died not of old age nor went out of the World by the ordinary ways of nature, but Famine & contagious Distempers, the Sword the Halter & a thousand mischiefs have consumed them. Yea of many of them perhaps Children were never born, for they that want means to nourish Children will abstain from Marriage or (which is all one) they cast away their Bodys upon rich old Women or otherwise make unequal or unhealthy Matches for gain, or because of poverty they think it a Blessing which in nature is a Curse to have their Wives barren.

"Were it not thus Arithmetical Progression might easily demonstrate how fast Mankind would increase in multitude overpassing (as miraculous tho' indeed natural) the Examples of the Israelites who were multiplied in 215 Years from 70 unto 600,000 able Men."[44] And Sir Josiah Child says "Such as our Employment is for People so many will our People be; & if we should imagine we have in England employment but for one hundred People & we have born & bred amongst us 150 People, I say the 50 must away from us or starve or be hanged to prevent it whether we had any foreign Plantations or not."[45]

Then if it be considered that our Plantations (spending mostly our English Manufactures and those of all sorts almost imaginable in egregious quantitys, and employing near two thirds of all our English Shipping) do therein give a constant sustenance to, it may be, two hundred thousand Persons here at home; I must needs conclude upon the whole matter, That we have not the fewer but the more People in England by reason of our English Plantations in America.

If the number of Inhabitants depends upon the quantity of Labour and that People increase proportionably as there is employment for them, then the increasing the demand of Manufactures will increase the people by giving work to so many Manufacturers as are employed in furnishing the Goods demanded. To explain this by Examples If 125 familys in England earn 2125 Pounds per Annum and those very familys by being removed into American shall earn 12325 Pounds per Annum the People of England will be increased by the removal of these familys for out of that 12325 Pounds 8216 Pounds will be spent in England to buy Tools, Cloaths, Arms etc. And 8216 Pounds spent in Goods will give employment to 410 People at 20 Pounds per Annum each and consequently support 410 Familys. It may be objected that what these People earned whilst in England should be taken off. Supposing that to be granted there will remain 6091 Pounds which will employ 304 Persons at 20 Pounds a Year each. So that the removal of 125 familys will give subsistance to and consequently increase the People of England by 304 Familys.

England imports to the value of two hundred thousand Pounds worth of raw Silk yearly from Italy. If these People should be able to furnish England with all the Silk it wants, then will they buy with that Silk 200,000 Pounds worth of such Goods as they want from England which will employ 10,000 Men at 20 Pounds each and consequently increase the People of England by 10,000 Familys. If they are employed in raising Hemp they will be able to furnish the Manufacturers of Britain and Ireland cheaper than they can be furnished from the East Sea or from any other part of the European Continent. The cheaper this material is in Britain and Ireland the more Manufacturers would be employed on it: for the consumption of Linnens would increase proportionably to the cheapness of the material since that would enable the Merchants to allow the Manufacturer a good price and yet undersell Foreigners in the Markets abroad: for at this present time all the Flax and Hemp growing in Britain and Ireland cannot keep all the Hands employed on the linnen Manufacture at work 3 Months in the Year.

As much as every Man earns by his labour so much does the Country he lives in get by him: therefore it is advantagious to a Kingdom that Men should be in that part of their Dominions where they can earn most. The labour of a white Man in South Carolina is worth at least 30 Pounds a Year; the labour of many of these poor (those who are in Prison particularly) cannot be worth 20 Shillings a Year. Supposing at an averidge that they should earn 6 Pounds a Year, a hundred of such Men in England would be but of 600 Pounds a Year value to the Kingdom. That 100 Men in Carolina where labour is worth 30 Pounds a Year would be worth 3,000 Pounds a Year to the Kingdom: nor would this

Money be to their advantage only, for he who earns there 30 Pounds a Year must wear Cloaths, use Tools Household Goods etc. to the value of 20 Pounds per Annum which he must buy from England, for they cannot make them there it not being worth their while who can earn 30 Pounds a Year upon raising Silk to lose their labour upon making Woolen Goods and Tools which are made by People who work for 15 Pounds a Year. If this then be the case

	£	S.	D.
A Man going to Carolina earns 30 Pounds a Year of which he spends for English Goods per Annum	20,	0,	0
This Man whilst he staid in England earned per Annum	6,	0,	0
The Kingdom gets by his removal	14,	0,	0

And the State, of which Carolina is part, gets the whole £30. And the Revenue gets the Dutys of those Goods with which he purchased the 20 Pounds worth of English Goods. To put this in a clearer light here follows a Scheme showing how much profit will arise to the Nation from the establishing one Colony only.

Loss to England by transporting 125 familys.	£	Gain by transporting Ditto.	£
25 of the best Men supposed to earn 15 Pounds per Annum each	375	25 of the best Men at 50 Pounds per Annum each	1250
100 poor Men at 6 Pounds Ditto	600	100 at 30 Pounds Ditto	3000
125 Women at Ditto	750	125 Women at 15 Pounds Ditto	1875
200 Children at 2 Pounds Ditto	400	200 Children at 6 Pounds Ditto	1200
	2125		7325

Supposing 50 Foreigners could be drawn from beyond
the Seas they at 30 Pounds a head would amount to   1500

8825

2125

Profit to England   6700

It seems to be pretty plainly proved that every foreigner and every English Man who cannot get work and goes to Carolina is a benefit to the Nation and increases the people: for he employs the Makers in England of all the English Goods he consumes and the more employment there is the more Manufacturers there will be.

The particular method we have laid down may vary according

as there shall be occasion: but that there may be a Colony success-
fully established is demonstrable. Under what difficultys was Virginia planted? the Coast and Climate were then unknown, the
Indians numerous and at enmety with the first Colony and they
were forced to fetch all Provisions from England. Yet they are
grown a mighty Province and the Revenue receives . . . for Dutys
upon the goods that they send yearly home.

Within this 50 Years Pensilvania was as much a Forrest as
Georgia is now and in those few Years by the wise Oeconomy of
William Penn and those who assisted him it now gives food to
thousands of Inhabitants and is the seat of as fine a City as most in
Europe.[46]

This Design is much more probable to succeed than either of
those were since Carolina abounds with Provisions the Climate is
known and there are Men to instruct in the Seasons and nature of
cultivating that Soil. Charles Town a great Mart is within 120
Miles: if the Colony is attacked it may be relieved from Sea by
Port Royal or the Bahamas and the Militia of South Carolina is
ready to support it by Land.[47]

There is an occasion now offered for every one to help forward
this Design. The smallest Benefactions will be received and applied with the utmost care, every little will do something and a
great number of small Benefactions will amount to a Sum capable
of doing a great deal of good.[48]

The time and occasion calls out upon the rich and generous
People of England. Religion, Charity and the love of our Countrey perswade, nay even self interest prompts to send away those
whom want may force against their own inclinations upon dangerous courses. Desperate poor never more abounded, a long
Peace has made evacuation necessary. Witness the frequent mur-
mures for want of employment from all parts of the Kingdom.
The Protestants from abroad harrassed by the madness of Romish

Priests, cry out for a place of refuge, the Vaudois the Polanders and the Germans would with joy enrich and strengthen your America. All Nations are improving their Trade all eager for foreign Plantations. Let not the Britons now grow indolent. All Nations are at peace take then the benefit of the general tranquility and improve beyond the Ocean. There without bloodshed or the hazard of a Battle you may increase the Wealth, the Strength and the honour of the Kingdom more than the Edwards or the Henrys did by their glorious but destructive Victorys. They burnt Towns, you will build them: they ravaged, you will cultivate large Dominions: They destroyed, you will preserve, and increase Mankind.

Finis

$\mathcal{N}$otes

INTRODUCTION

1. Robert Johnson to James Edward Oglethorpe, September 28, 1732, in *Colonial Records of the State of Georgia*, Allen D. Candler, Kenneth Coleman, et al., eds., 31 vols. to date (Atlanta and Athens, 1904–), 20: 2–3.

2. See Thomas Christie, "The Voyage of the *Anne* – A Daily Record," ed. Robert G. McPherson, *Georgia Historical Quarterly* 44 (1960): 224; Peter Gordon, *The Journal of Peter Gordon, 1732–1735*, ed. E. Merton Coulter (Athens, 1963), 28.

3. See especially Rodney M. Baine and Mary E. Williams, "Oglethorpe's Early Military Campaigns," *Yale University Library Gazette* 60 (1985): 63–76; Rodney M. Baine, "James Oglethorpe and the Early Promotional Literature for Georgia," *William and Mary Quarterly*, 3d series, 45 (1988): 100–106; and Baine, "The Prison Death of Robert Castell and Its Effect on the Founding of Georgia," *Georgia Historical Quarterly* 73 (1989): 67–78. See also Baine and Williams, "James Oglethorpe in Europe: Recent Findings in His Military Career," in *Oglethorpe in Perspective: Georgia's Founder After Two Hundred Years*, Phinizy Spalding and Harvey H. Jackson, eds. (Tuscaloosa, 1989), 112–21. For other recent insights into Oglethorpe's activities see Louis De Vorsey, Jr., "Oglethorpe and the Earliest Maps of Georgia," *Oglethorpe in Perspective*, 22–43; and Milton L. Ready, "Philanthropy and the Origins of Georgia," *Forty Years of Diversity: Essays on Colonial Georgia*, Jackson and Spalding, eds. (Athens, 1984), 46–59.

4. "A Latin Poem by James Edward Oglethorpe," contributed by

Rudolf Kirk, *Georgia Historical Quarterly* 32 (1948): 29–31; Phinizy Spalding, "Oglethorpe and Johnson: A Cordial Connection," *Johnson Society Transactions* (December 1974): 52–61.

5. See *A Catalogue of the Entire and Valuable Library of General Oglethorpe* (London, 1785) for verification of his holdings.

6. Oglethorpe's account of this war gives it the proper menace that most who lived through it felt. For years the dangers posed to South Carolina were downplayed. The possible results of such a war, allying the natives and the blacks against the minority whites, were simply too horrible to articulate, so that direct contemporary references to the Yamasee uprisings are relatively few. Only with the publication of Peter Wood's *Black Majority: Negroes in Colonial South Carolina from 1670 Through the Stono Rebellion* (New York, 1974) have the hostilities in all their fury been adequately described; see especially pp. 128–30.

7. On land speculation in South Carolina see M. Eugene Sirmans, *Colonial South Carolina: A Political History, 1663–1763* (Chapel Hill, 1966), 10–12, 30–39, 50–54, 62–64, 170–82, passim, and Richard P. Sherman, *Robert Johnson: Proprietary and Royal Governor of South Carolina* (Columbia, S.C., 1966).

8. Phinizy Spalding, *Oglethorpe in America* (Chicago, 1977), 10–12, 84–87, 90–91, 94–97, passim.

9. See *Colonial Records of Georgia*, 1:31–54 for the three acts passed by the Georgia Trustees during their tenure.

10. Oglethorpe to the Trustees, June 9, 1733, Phillipps Collection of Egmont Papers, Hargrett Rare Book and Manuscript Library, University of Georgia Libraries, 14200:83. After refusing the Carolinians' demands for slavery and large land grants, Oglethorpe commented that perhaps he "should [have] kicked the proposers into the Bargain."

11. See particularly Betty Wood, "Thomas Stephens and the Introduction of Black Slavery in Georgia," *Georgia Historical Quarterly* 58 (1974): 24–40, and the same author's *Slavery in Colonial Georgia, 1730–1775* (Athens, 1984), 44–58.

12. Clearly the best article on the background of the Savannah plan is by John Reps, "$C^2 + L^2 = S^2$? Another Look at the Origins of Savan-

nah's Town Plan," in *Forty Years of Diversity*, 101–51, but even this prop- osition is conjectural.

13. Harvey H. Jackson, "Parson and Squire: James Oglethorpe and the Role of the Anglican Church in Georgia, 1733–1736," in *Oglethorpe in Perspective*, 44–65, provides a clear analysis of Oglethorpe's notion of where ecclesiastical affairs rested in relation to secular, at least on the American scene.

14. Betty Wood, "James Edward Oglethorpe, Race, and Slavery," *Oglethorpe in Perspective*, 70.

15. For development of the idea of Georgia as a purified secular state, see Spalding, "James Edward Oglethorpe's Quest for an American Zion," *Forty Years of Diversity*, 60–79.

16. It was first noted, briefly quoted, and ascribed to Martyn by Mills B. Lane III in the third edition of his *Savannah Revisited* (Savannah, 1977), 43. It was discussed, quoted in greater length, and similarly at- tributed by John Reps in "$C^2 + L^2 = S^2$?" 117, 120, 148–49 n. 21. It was first attributed to Oglethorpe by Rodney M. Baine in "James Oglethorpe and the Early Promotional Literature," 100–106.

17. The paper shows the "Maid of Dort" watermark, almost identical with Churchill 134, which William Algernon Churchill dates as approx- imately 1732 in his *Watermarks in Paper in Holland, England, France, etc. in the Seventeenth and Eighteenth Centuries* (Amsterdam, 1935; repr. Rej- swijk, 1965), c, 71.

18. There is no coronet here, and the two helmets above a single garb become in the bookplate two garbs above a single helmet.

19. The collation follows: title page, verso blank; Preface, tén leaves, the first three unpaginated, then seven leaves incorrectly paginated 4 to 16; the text, forty-six leaves, paginated 1 to 92, with the number 90 omit- ted in paginating, the final page blank. Penciled on page 1 of the text is the number 20, and on page 33, the number 51. A leaf has been torn out after page 4 of the text, but there is no hiatus there.

20. *Manuscripts of the Earl of Egmont: Diary of Viscount Percival*, ed. R. A. Roberts. Historical Manuscripts Commission 3 vols. (London, 1920– 23), 1:286.

21. Associates of Dr. Bray, "Minute Book, 1729[1730]–1732," Archives of Society for the Propagation of the Gospel in Foreign Parts, London (microfilm, Library of Congress), 36:23. See also Albert B. Saye, *New Viewpoints in Georgia History* (Athens, 1943), 16 n. 31. For a discussion of the Bray Associates, see Verner W. Crane, "Dr. Thomas Bray and the Charitable Colony Project," *William and Mary Quarterly*, 3d series, 19 (1962): 49–63.

22. Bray "Minute Book," 36.

23. Ibid., 27.

24. Percival, *Diary*, 1:219.

25. Bray "Minute Book," 50–51.

26. James Oglethorpe, ed., *Select Tracts Relating to Colonies* (London, 1732), iv–v; *South Carolina Gazette*, March 23, 1733; *Library of Oglethorpe*, items 503, 717, 1160, 2113, and 2350 — editions of 1701, 1687, 1677, 1614, and 1736. Probably only one copy would have satisfied the Reverend Mr. Thomas Pollen, another Corpus Christi man, whose library was apparently sold along with Oglethorpe's. Another example of Oglethorpe's veneration for, and identification with, Raleigh seems to occur when he misinterprets Tomochichi's story of a red-bearded visitor to the Savannah River many years before. Although it must have been Ribault, Oglethorpe wants to believe it is Raleigh, even though the Elizabethan adventurer never stopped on the coast of Spanish Guale. For information on this point see Peter Wood's essay in *Oglethorpe in Perspective*, 5–21.

27. *Select Tracts*, 5–17; *The Works of Nicholas Machiavel*, trans. Ellis Farneworth (London, 1680); *Library of Oglethorpe*, item 1864.

28. *Select Tracts*, 31–40; *Library of Oglethorpe*, item 791 or 1111.

29. *Calendar of State Papers. Colonial Series. America and West Indies*, 44 vols. to date (London, 1860–), 39:32 (hereafter designated *CSP*); *Journal of the Commissioners for Trade and Plantations*, 14 vols. (London, 1920–38), 6:316.

30. See *The Country Journal, or Craftsman*, (February 5, 1732), p. 2; *London Evening Post*, (February 5, 1732), p. 1.

31. *CSP*, 38:217–19.

32. In Herman Moll's *New and Exact Map of the Dominions of the King*

of Great Britain, on the Continent of North America, there is an inset map of the southern region showing "GEORGIA" between the Savannah and the Altamaha rivers. Though the first state of the large map was engraved in 1715, the state with the inset, sold by Bowles, was dated conjecturally as 1731 by *Research Catalog of Maps of America to 1860 in the William L. Clements Library,* Douglas W. Marshall, ed. (Boston, 1972), 2:96. The *National Union Catalog,* however, places the Bowles imprint in 1732, surely the earliest possible date for the use of the new name by a cartographer. Webb Garrison has commented upon this mistaken date in his *Oglethorpe's Folly: The Birth of Georgia* (Lakemont, 1982), 229–30 n. 9. Similarly misleading is the date of Mark Catesby's reference to "that Province honour'd with the name of *Georgia,*" in the preface to his *Natural History of Carolina, Florida, and the Bahama Islands* (1729), 1:x. Though dated 1731 on the title page, the first volume consists of the preface and five fascicles, the first issued in 1729, the last on November 23, 1732 — the earliest possible date for the preface. See George F. Frick, "Mark Catesby," *Papers of the Bibliographical Society of America* 54 (1960): 170.

33. Belcher to Coram, December 9, 1731, *Belcher Papers,* in *Collections of the Massachusetts Historical Society,* 6th series (Boston, 1886–99), 6:86–87.

34. Bray "Minute Book," 55.

35. Like his contemporaries, Oglethorpe frequently used the word "colony" to denote a single settlement and "colonies," a group of settlements, like Savannah, Augusta, Frederica, and Darien. His use of "Colonys" in his title suggests only a series of settlements.

36. *CSP*, 37:384.

37. Percival, *Diary*, 1:193, 226–27.

38. *Berkeley and Percival: The Correspondence of George Berkeley and Sir John Percival,* ed. Benjamin Rand (Cambridge, 1914), 277.

39. Percival, *Diary*, 1:265.

40. *Colonial Records of Georgia*, 20:1–2.

41. Ibid., 2:43–45.

42. Percival, *Diary*, 1:293.

43. Belcher to Coram, April 24, 1732, and December 9, 1731, in *Belcher Papers*, 6:112, 87.

44. Percival, *Diary*, 1:289. The minutes of neither the Common Council nor the Trustees record this action, but it is confirmed in the *Journal of the Earl of Egmont*, ed. Robert G. McPherson (Atlanta, 1962), 5. Note that Percival reproduced Oglethorpe's "Design" rather than Martyn's "Designs."

45. *Colonial Records of Georgia*, 2:3.

SOME ACCOUNT OF THE DESIGN OF THE TRUSTEES
FOR ESTABLISHING COLONYS IN AMERICA

1. The Phocaeans founded Massilia (Marseilles) as a trading station but settled at Elea, in Italy.

2. Homer's *Odyssey*, Alexander Pope translation, 6.9–16. Apparently Oglethorpe, whose *Library* shows no copy of this translation, left his amanuensis to locate the passage: the scribe left almost two pages for it but used less than a page.

3. In these two paragraphs Oglethorpe probably follows either Raleigh's *History*, 5.1.2, or Thucydides' *The History of the Peloponnesian War*, 6.3.1, of which the *Library of Oglethorpe* shows the 1696 edition, item 1201; the Hobbes translation of 1676, item 209; and the 1721 translation of William Smith, item 1309.

4. Oglethorpe neglects to add that because of differences about command the ships were not dispatched. See Raleigh's *History*, 5.1.3, or Herodotus, *Histories*, 7.158–63.

5. In this paragraph Oglethorpe echoes the suggestions of Charles Davenant in his "Discourse on the Plantation Trade." See *The Political and Commercial Works of Charles Davenant* (London, 1771; repr. Farnborough, Eng., 1967), 2:4–8. The city "called the Italian" was Italica.

6. Oglethorpe follows Appian's *Roman History*, 6.7.38.

7. Oglethorpe employs the political arithmetic that he apparently learned from William Petty, Sir Josiah Child, and Charles Davenant. He had already used it in his *Sailor's Advocate*.

8. Oglethorpe quotes from Appian's *Roman History*, 1.1.7 and

2.19.140, possibly translating into English his 1670 edition, in Greek and Latin (*Library*, item 912). The reference to Brutus's oration also derives from Appian, 2.19.140.

9. In his letter of May 1731 to George Berkeley, Oglethorpe wrote, "The merely releasing them they thought an imperfect charity, since those only who had friends to put them in a way of subsistence could reap a real benefit from it, since others whose credit, health, and perhaps morals, were impaired by a prison could have no advantage from the Act, but the privilege of starving at large" (Rand, *Berkeley and Percival*, 276–77). The final phrase reappears in Benjamin Martyn's *Reasons*, 25.

10. Following this paragraph is the penciled direction "go to pag 29." Oglethorpe refers to the death by starvation and fever that he and his committee found at the Marshalsea Prison in 1730.

11. This paragraph, on page 29 of the manuscript, is marked for removal by a penciled marginal line and the direction "Leeve out heer and incert in p. 3."

12. Sir Walter Raleigh, *A Discourse of . . . War* (London, 1650), D4v–D[5]r.

13. Captain Coram was to become the father of the Foundling Hospital; on April 2, 1730, Oglethorpe was appointed to the committee concerned with the care of bastard children (*Journals of the House of Commons* [London, n.d.], 21:524). But this concern for vagrant children characterized all the Bray Associates. On May 11, 1732, some of them framed a parliamentary motion "for addressing his majesty to give a sum not exceeding 10,000*l.* for binding vagrants and beggars out apprentices at 10*l.* per head, and to allow masters 20*l.* for every four apprentices he should take, and to settle them in Carolina" (Percival, *Diary*, 1:273). The petition was, however, modified and delayed; and it finally died (Percival, *Diary*, 1:274, 276; *JHC*, 21:921, 925). Sir Josiah Child had suggested such a measure in his *New Discourse*, 67.

14. The Port Royal River is now called the Broad River.

15. There follows a caret, and in the margin is penciled the direction "incert Page 11." The sentence there underlined for transferral, we have incorporated but have not italicized here.

16. At the end of this paragraph is penciled the direction "incert Page

15 to Pag. 19." This paragraph and the following, which begins "Beyond South Edistow," are set off by inked marginal rules.

17. By the time Oglethorpe wrote his *New and Accurate Account* he had acquired a copy of John Archdale's *New Description of that Fertile and Pleasant Province of Carolina* (London, 1717). Here, however, he quotes Archdale secondhand, from John Oldmixon, *The British Empire in America* (London, 1708), 1:276–77.

18. Oldmixon, *British Empire*, 1:378. The italicized paragraphs were penciled for removal, by marginal lines, then crossed out. The introductory paragraph is also adapted from Oldmixon.

19. Of this sentence, penciled in the margin, we cannot be absolutely certain of the last two words.

20. Savannah Town, across the river from the site of the future Augusta, had been deserted for some time.

21. Fort King George, near present Darien, was established by South Carolina in 1721 but burned in late 1725 and was abandoned in 1728. Placed at the forks of the Altamaha on John Herbert's map of 1725, the fort was actually built on the northernmost stream of the river's mouth, close to the site of an earlier Spanish mission. At the forks of the Altamaha a small trader's fort had succeeded the ephemeral Spanish outpost of Tama.

22. Mark Catesby's *Natural History* (1729–47), in which Oglethorpe is listed as a subscriber. Doubtless Oglethorpe acquired a good deal of information about the region from sources like Catesby; Paul Amatis; Sir Alexander Cuming, who returned to London from there in 1730 with a party of Cherokees; Governor Robert Johnson, a long-time resident who was in England during most of 1730; Jean Pierre Purry, whom Oglethorpe met in England in 1731; and the seven Cherokees also. He knew their host, Thomas Arne, the father of the famous composer Thomas Augustine Arne.

23. Of our reading "Jetting" we cannot be certain. Beginning with "Excepting" the latter part of the sentence is penciled between lines, then in the margin.

24. Oglethorpe refers to Paul Amatis, who had already visited South Carolina and who returned with him and the first Georgia settlers.

25. Thomas Boreman's *Compendious Account of the Whole Art of Breeding, Nursing, and the Right Ordering of the Silk-worm* (London, 1732), dedicated to Percival and the Georgia Trustees. For details on this promotional pamphlet, see Rodney M. Baine, "James Oglethorpe and the Early Promotional Literature," 106.

26. Martyn borrowed here for his *Some Account*, 3, and his *Reasons*, 28.

27. From here and the previous paragraph, Martyn quoted and paraphrased in *Some Account*, 1, and *Reasons*, 26.

28. Here the scribe left almost two pages blank, evidently for the insertion of a passage from Machiavelli's *History of Florence*, probably for one of the sections from book 2 that Oglethorpe later incorporated in his *Select Tracts*.

29. This sentence is inked at the bottom of an otherwise blank page, with no indication of where it should be placed.

30. The latter part of this paragraph and the following sentence are quoted and paraphrased in Martyn's *Some Account*, 2.

31. A quite similar statement appeared in *The Daily Post* on February 6, 1732.

32. The latter part of this paragraph Martyn quoted and paraphrased in *Some Account*, 4.

33. Of this sentence, penciled in the margin, the reading is partly conjectural. Presumably the Trustees would accept some proposals and would inquire into the characters of those who submitted them.

34. Boreman's pamphlet on sericulture. In the margin the amanuensis inked the query "?where."

35. In 1722 John Montagu, second duke of Montagu, was granted the islands of St. Vincent and St. Lucia, but his attempted landing was repulsed by the Spaniards.

36. The letter to Berkeley promises to provide the poor families "passage, clothes, arms, working tools, &c., and provisions for one year" (Rand, *Berkeley and Percival*, 277).

37. The letter to Berkeley reads, "In return of the money laid out upon them, of their being rescued from poverty, and instead of rent for their lands each man is to give one day's labour in six, which day's labour is to be employed on lands to be reserved for the use of the charity. Out

of the produce of those public lands the aged and the sick are to be subsisted, and the people to be supported in case of the casualties of famine, pestilence, or war; and if there shall be any remainder it is to be applied by the Society to the sending over more poor families" (Ibid., 278).

38. Oglethorpe's feudal ideal of moral and legal responsibility was present in the initial ideal as he expounded it to Percival on February 13, 1730. The settlers, he explained, would "be subject to subordinate rulers, who should inspect their behaviour and labour under one chief head" (Percival, *Diary*, 1:45).

39. There follows a long quotation from Vitruvius, *De Architectura*, evidently in Robert Castell's advertised but unpublished translation, 1.4.1–2, 7–9, 11–12; 1.5.1; 1.6.1, 3. The long dashes indicate omissions.

40. Oglethorpe quotes Raleigh's *History*, 3.7.1. The quotation actually begins with the ampersand.

41. Compare the letter to Berkeley in Rand, *Berkeley and Percival*, 277.

42. In his letter to Benjamin Martyn on February 12, 1733, Governor Johnson admitted, "I did propose the Subsisting them with Provisions for a twelve month, but the Charge has been so great already with the Purisburgers . . . that the Assembly thought the Expense too large" (*Colonial Records of Georgia*, 20:11).

43. Compare Martyn's *Short Account*, 2–3.

44. Raleigh's *Discourse*, D[5]v–D[6]r.

45. Sir Josiah Child, "A Discourse Concerning Plantations," in *A New Discourse of Trade* (London, 1693), 174.

46. Martyn quotes this paragraph and the preceding one in *Reasons*, 28.

47. This sentence, with an added clause, appears in Martyn's *Reasons*, 28.

48. Martyn quotes this paragraph in *Some Account*, 4, and paraphrases from the previous four paragraphs in *Some Account*, 3–4.